The Growing Tree of Life Inside Us

Gifts Within Our Soul

By Inocencia Tupas Malunes

I create mine and share, so you can create what you wish and love to do

◆ FriesenPress

One Printers Way
Altona, MB R0G 0B0
Canada

www.friesenpress.com

Copyright © 2021 by Inocencia Tupas Malunes
First Edition — 2021

All rights reserved.

No part of this publication may be reproduced in any form, or by any means, electronic or mechanical, including photocopying, recording, or any information browsing, storage, or retrieval system, without permission in writing from FriesenPress.

ISBN
978-1-03-912184-3 (Hardcover)
978-1-03-912183-6 (Paperback)
978-1-03-912185-0 (eBook)

1. BODY, MIND & SPIRIT, INSPIRATION & PERSONAL GROWTH

Distributed to the trade by The Ingram Book Company

Table of Contents

Chapter 1 – Finding the Real Self 1

Chapter 2 – When Mind and Body are Connected 7

Chapter 3 – Making a Bright Future 13

Chapter 4 – Born Again by the Spirit 17

Chapter 5 – Experience the Fullness of Life 23

Chapter 6 – Think and Grow Rich 27

Chapter 7 – Giving First and the Getting Follows 31

Chapter 8 – Become Clear in Life 37

Chapter 9 – From Old to the New 47

Chapter 10 – Follow Your Heart, Believe in Yourself 53

Chapter 11 – I Did Not Choose This Job, the Job Chose Me 59

Chapter 12 – The Magic of Life Is Living Itself 65

Chapter 13 – Become a Master of Your Own Thoughts 69

Chapter 14 – Forgiveness and Forgetfulness 73
Chapter 15 – This Is the End of Being Selfish 77
Chapter 16 – Standing on Our Own Two Feet 81
Chapter 17 – How to Find Freedom 83
Chapter 18 – Practical Knowledge 85
Chapter 19 – Create Something That Will Last Our Lifetime.... 87
Chapter 20 – Friends and Foes Are All the Same 91
Chapter 21 – Recognize "Me" 93
Chapter 22 – Respecting the Rights of One Another 97
Chapter 23 – Taste These Blessings Yourself 99
Chapter 24 – All One in Spirit 101
Chapter 25 – The Truth That Has Been Revealed to Me 103
Chapter 26 – Please Don't Harm Anyone Great or Small 107

Dedication

I dedicate this book to my parents, who brought me into this world so that I could walk here during this lifetime. To my siblings and my husband, who participate in my existence. We all work together to survive and become "One."

Chapter 1 – Finding the Real Self

The unfoldment of my unconsciousness to my consciousness occurred one morning when my husband, Fermin, and I were having breakfast. Out of nowhere, I started crying for no reason at all. I can't explain how it started, but I just cried nonstop, as if something inside of me had died. The food in front of me was full of my tears, and Fermin didn't know what to do.

"Stop it," he said. "What's wrong with you?"

It lasted for almost ten minutes, and afterwards it seemed like nothing had happened, except I'd felt something cleanse me. I felt so light, as though a ton of rocks had dropped from my shoulders. I could see clearly now. I didn't feel worry, sadness, or fear of bad things happening—just appreciation of the beauty that surrounded me in life.

Life is so simple and easy, but if we're not yet awakened to the truth, we think that life must be tough. But you can quiet your mind and know who you really are. Yes, you can, but only through your heart, which is the gateway to life and to where the mansion of your heavenly Father. There, life is magical, and everything you touch comes to life easily. Once you accept that you and your Father in heaven are one, and meditate on that, you will feel the love flowing through you and out to others that you meet.

It is the I Am and the me that we call "I Am." And you thought it was "us"? The higher intelligence, the higher being inside us all, is our "real self," or consciousness, that when unfolded and connected to the universal consciousness is the energy from all that is, the invisible and visible that has life. We are all energy. Nothing is dead but only an energy that changes form. We can't see it, but it's there. Once we reach this level of consciousness, our perception of things changes, and all we can see are the positives and no negatives anymore. We exist in the third dimension, but if we awaken, we can access different dimensions. There's a lower and middle dimension, where we all grew, and there are higher dimensions—the fourth, fifth, sixth, seventh, and so on. That's why in other teachings, people are more advanced in their knowledge of the chakras in our bodies where the flow of energy can move through easily. Chakras are part of the main organs of our body's likes the sex organ, the stomach, the plexus the heart the neck and so on to the crown chakras which is on the top of our heads When that happens, our lives are in harmony with the flow of energy from the universal consciousness, were all life energy exists.

I never have to think too hard about what I'm doing. Whether I'm cooking or cleaning, it all seems effortless, and I finish quickly. I don't even have to think about how I'll get the supplies I need—they just come to me with no effort. I don't know how it happens or why. I don't question anymore; all I know is that I'm not me anymore, meaning my ego self. That crying event was about cleansing my old ways. I can't go back to my old ways, no matter how much I try. It was unbalanced, with too much giving without receiving.

I just finished writing my first book yesterday, and here I am writing again. I love doing it, but no matter how hard I tried to write before, I just couldn't. I can't explain why, but now all I can say is that I did it, and I did it for me.

The Growing Tree of Life Inside Us

I don't know how long my life here will last, as it's not in my keeping. All I can do is give as much happiness, joy, and gratitude that I can to our humanity and the care of our planet. We all must contribute for our own survival and our future generations.

My writing will focus on building awareness of what we're all doing to our lives when we destroy ourselves by the useless killing of one another in the name of religion. We must wake up now for the sake of our younger generation. We must guide them to do the right thing for their survival and the survival of all that is. We don't like to live in boxes, separated from each other. How can we be separate when we are all one, connected to one another as part of the universal consciousness. I met a lady the other day and we start chatting. She asked me if I was familiar with the term "rhyme zone." I didn't have a clue what that was, so she said, "You are one of my other selves."

Please think before it's too late. We must look after one another, especially our brothers and sisters who are weak and vulnerable. We must speak up to protect them. One morning on our walk, I found myself talking with a person sleeping on the street. I asked his name, and he said his name was Simon. I asked him how old he was, and he said "thirty."

"What happened?" I asked. "Did you forget who you are? While you're lying down there, talk to the deepest core of your heart and he will remind you of who you really are."

He laughed at me, and I told him not to laugh but to do what I'd said, and his inner self would change him. I told him that he could have a better life and that he deserved it. I gave him ten dollars and left.

Three days later, we passed by the same spot and saw a note that said, "I am homeless, but not hopeless." I never saw him again. Even taking a bit of time to say something kind can be a big encouragement to the needy. Don't laugh at people's physical appearance. That's the body they chose to experience in this lifetime. Your soul will pick your body, face, and height. What you laugh at right now could be what you pick to experience in your next lifetime, so please think and be considerate to others. Remember the saying: "The I Am in others is also the I Am in you." We help one another in disasters, accidents, and calamities because we aren't separate from one another and everything that is. But most of us are not awakened to the meaning of being one in spirit. If you don't want to talk, a smile is better than a cold face, don't you think? And it's not heavy to carry. Give it freely, and it will come back to you a hundred-fold.

My life has changed completely. My outlook is different, and my old ways are in the past. The happiness and endless joy inside of me is hard to explain, but I want others to have the same experience and the courage to write about how they feel. There are no more cravings, just the feeling of fullness of fulfillment. My brothers and sisters, begin your meditation from within yourself. Through your hearts, slowly knock on the door and feel that he hears you, whatever you believe in. He is there just waiting for you to recognize him and be one with him. Don't separate from him or her, because we are all one. He, or she, are you, and you are or him, or her. If only you recognize and believe, you won't be empty-handed.

To begin, just be quiet for two minutes. Any time will do. Just stop whatever you're doing, be still, and say, "I am God" in a very serious way. Repeat it as many times as you can and make it a habit, for sooner or later, you will become as you think in your hearts. It's the truth, and you can prove it to yourself. Please do it. It won't harm you but will build you up. Trust me, I've done it.

No one can change you but you, and only if you want to. If you don't like your situation, then switch your thinking. It's as simple as that. Free yourself from the bondage of worries, sadness, fear, anxieties, problems, they are only in your thoughts; they aren't real, so stop thinking about it. It's as simple as that, and that's what freedom is all about.

How long are you going to maintain the state of mind that doesn't give you any joy or happiness? When you feel joyful and happy, you

The Growing Tree of Life Inside Us

can think easier and do good things to improve your life. You can also teach others to do the same and triple the effect. That's how the whole world will be brighter. We need to build up, not destroy, one another. I never raised a child of my own, but I learned how to look after the children of others with care, love, and respect, and I'm good at that. Their parents are thankful to me. Their children are grown up, happy and with their own families. How good is that?

Now that you have this understanding, don't you want that kind of life? Where joy and happiness are abundant? Don't worry about your riches being taken away from you when you die. You will not die, but your ego will, and you won't feel hunger or thirst anymore. You won't feel want any more, but you'll feel fulfilled. You are still here. Don't be afraid, because the best is yet to come. All your anger, anxiety, worry, fear, and sadness will disappear without you noticing it. Your life will be so different from what it used to be. Things will be easier, and you won't need to think so hard. You will be in touch with your inner knowing and understanding. Isn't that beautiful?

You may think you're not ready for this, but don't worry. The time will come, and your doubt will disappear. We are the new visionary, the new voice, the new co-creator of our environment. We are all multidimensional and a collective group. We can create a cleaner earth for the coming re-generation in this planet.

Can you imagine living in harmony, where nobody wears a sour face but everyone is smiling? Wouldn't that be amazing? Yes, we are all capable of that, and who will prevent us when we're living in the light as one.

Chapter 2 – When Mind and Body are Connected

One day I was on the bus and a beautiful lady stood up quickly to offer her seat to me.

"Sit down, dear," I said. "You paid your fare too."

She smiled at me and said she'd offered the seat because I was older than her, so I sat down. Then the gentleman beside me stood up and offered his seat to her, so she sat down beside me. She introduced herself as Michelle, and I told her that was a pretty name. I said that my name was, but she couldn't quite pronounce it. As we talked, she told me that something different was going on inside of her, and she'd never felt this way before. She was only twenty-one years old.

She had been born in South Africa and now lived in Vancouver. I told her not to be afraid of what was happening to her, because it was about the awakening of many people due to the high energy of our planet. It was affecting more people, including me. I told her not to fear because she was on the right path of finding her higher self, her divine self. The higher intelligence is one, and that's our real selves.

Another beautiful young woman walked toward me one day as I was standing by the street. She was carrying a small pamphlet that she gave to me. "These are the words of God," she said. "Be awake."

"Are you awake?" I asked. "Of who you are? You and God are one. I am you, and you in me."

Her eyes went wide and she said that no one had ever told her that.

"Now you know," I said. After that, I never saw her again.

Last month, I was talking to my nephew's wife, Rosalie, on the phone, and I asked her about my sister, Rosalinda. She said that my sister and her husband had gone to the hospital because they were throwing up and didn't know why. I had often told my sister that if she ever felt strange suddenly for no reason, to go to the hospital and be monitored by the nurses.

While at the hospital, their blood pressure was up They stayed there for four hours until it got down to normal. After that, all was well. They stopped throwing up as if nothing had happened. I told them to meditate before going to bed and in the morning before doing anything else. It's just like saying your prayers, except you close your eyes and don't think of anything. Just quiet your mind and focus on your breathing. Do that every day and then one day it will happen—you will get some idea and the message will be loud and clear. Just open your heart by feeling love, happiness, and joy, not worry or sadness. Remember the days when you were young and the things you enjoyed doing. You felt so happy to just go with the flow of life given to you by the universe. One day you will understand what I'm talking about, because it can happen. They are happening to them now, and they found the truth of what I told them.

My younger brothers and sisters, things are happening to many people now, and earth is changing, as we are, so be prepared for it to happen to you. It's the beginning of a new, beautiful, happy, and easy life. You will know it when it comes, and you will be thankful to me for telling you in advance. Some call it your Saturn return it means that this planet complete around the orbit every twenty nine years and it's the one checking how we spend our life time here on earth, If we don't do well it keeps us moving on the right direction.

The Growing Tree of Life Inside Us

Yesterday morning during our walk, Fermin was way ahead of me. I was noticing every little thing I passed, from the little blossom of tiny flowers on the side of the road to the changing of the different trees. It popped into my mind that it's been a while since Fermin had traveled home, so I suggested to him that we visit his family for three weeks. I had to push, because he doesn't like to travel. He was quiet for a while and then said, "Why not?" I didn't wait a second. I called the travel agency and booked a flight to Madrid, Spain for October.

I like going to Spain that time of the year because the chestnut trees are full of fruit, and the wild mushrooms are everywhere up the mountain. I'm amazed at the beauty of the place. The mountains and green trees are so inspiring, especially driving around the winding road up by the hills and different shapes of mountains. It's so inviting. Whenever I hear of a friend traveling to Spain, I always suggest going to Asturias in the north of Spain. There we visited so many beautiful churches that I could feel the living Christ alive and well in me and all the people I met. I hope they could feel him inside of themselves as well.

We often ask ourselves: What is my purpose in life? Mine is to be happy and joyful, to add to the beauty of life. I've had a glimpse of the importance of why I am here on this earth for this lifetime. I have been doing it since I started earning money working for a living. I don't focus on spending it on myself but always help my family and other people who I know need it the most. During my younger years, I didn't have any savings of my own, but my needs were always met. I always had a job, and if I didn't like it, I improved my skills and found other works. I studied at community college in the evening while working during the day. It seemed so easy, even though I lived on my own when I came to Canada. I didn't have a difficult time managing my life. I never say to myself that life is tough, because for me, it's always been easy to make a living.

Now that I'm growing in my consciousness, I know exactly why I'm here on this beautiful earth in this lifetime. It's so clear now to me, and I'm following it wherever it leads. I am who I am, and I just open my heart to love for my younger brothers and sisters.

Have courage in your situation right now, and don't give up, whatever trials you are in. Because that's the road to success. I've been there before, and now I'm here telling you the truth of my life as I find my real and only self: "ME."

Do you have the courage to find the real you? Your real self? The higher intelligence inside of you that is the real and only self you have? The "I am and the me" in you? If you have the courage to believe that you are one with it, you will be surprised at the magic of life you will learn from will be able to access anything you want, especially your inner gifts to do what you want to do in life. You can do it all.

The inspiration that is flowing to you is nonstop, and it brings you to higher vibrations that make you excited about doing the things you love. This will spur you on into action, which will bring results. First the idea, then the choice and decision, and then the action and fruition.

We used to be limited to a very tight space, but as we grow, it becomes wider and we have more room to move and maneuver. We don't need others to tell us what to do because we have that knowledge already. All the tools are inside of us. But until we really know who we are, we can't access them. So, my brothers and sisters, always remember the words in the old teaching, "Know thyself." Everyone can access this through their hearts because whatever and whoever you believe you are, you will become.

Meditation is must. Quieting your mind is so important to having the clear message of your real self. Your higher self, the higher intelligence, is one, and it's the real and only self you have: "you and me." From now on, don't separate yourself from "God," for we are all one. We are all gods. At first it's difficult to convince your ego of this. It will try to force you not to believe it, because it's fighting for its

The Growing Tree of Life Inside Us

life. But as you continue and insist on the truth, the magic of your life will begin.

I examined my beliefs when I was twenty-one years old. If it didn't give me happiness and abundant life, I questioned it. I desired to find out the truth, and it was revealed to me. My brothers and sisters, the words in the old books of teaching, "Ask and it will be given unto you, knock and it will be open unto you," have been proven by me. With authority, I now reveal the truth to you, because it's happened to me. That's why I write this—to reveal to you the happiness and endless joy I feel inside of me. I want you all to experience it while you're still in the flesh, because heaven isn't a place that you find somewhere. It's "inside" of us where we find truth, happiness, and joy. You can have it here on this earth, and everything will be added unto you. If your life is happy and joyful, you can do many good things here on earth. You can create the beautiful life you want to live, and you can share your love and abundant life with those who are less fortunate. You can share your knowledge with those who are ready to accept it for their own good.

Once your mind and body are connected, the flow of energy continues without blockage. It's easy for you to do or create whatever you came here for. The sooner you open your gift, the more time you'll have to enjoy it and prosper with it.

Chapter 3 – Making a Bright Future

When I was younger I often asked my mother if I could sleep over at my aunt's house to hear her fairy tale stories. She told me so many stories, but the one that stuck with me was about three fairy sisters having a bath in the river. They were enjoying it very much, but they didn't know that a hunter was watching them. After a long time, the two older ones asked their younger sister if she was ready to go. She was enjoying it so much that she told them she wanted to stay longer, so the two other sisters left without her. The hunter took her clothes and hid them.

When young fairy finished swimming, she looked for her clothes but couldn't find them. She started crying, and the hunter came from out of his hiding place and offered her his jacket if she would go with him to his house. She had no choice but to go with him and become his wife. They eventually had a son. He was a handsome boy, and she took care of him very well. But one day her son was crying, and she couldn't make him stop. Because her husband was a hunter, the two of them were alone in the house.

She wondered why her son was looking up at the ceiling, so she climbed up on the roof of their house and found a small bamboo tube where all her clothes had been hidden by her husband. When she came back down, her son died. Then she put on her clothes and flew away. And that's the end of the story.

I don't know why this story made me so excited even when my aunt told it for the hundredth time. I never got tired of hearing it; it inspired me. I'm who I am today because of that story. Maybe because it's about freedom, but I don't know. Every time I visit my home country, I remind my aunt about that story. She says she can't remember it. Each of us has some kind of fairy tale we heard when we were growing up that we keep inside ourselves. They inspire us to survive our life situations and form us into what we become, and whether we are successful or not when we grow up.

Inspiration, desire, courage, and action lead to success and a bright future. Sometimes we get discouraged when we fail, but once you know who you really are, everything you want just flows to you because it's already the will of your higher self. Whatever you love to do will come to fruition.

We are spirit, and spirit is energy. Energy never dies—it just changes form. Be careful what you wish for, whether negative or positive, because it will come to you when you awaken to your spirituality. You can't misstep because you are always guided by the universe. You can call it any name you want, but it's all one, and that's the truth.

As you can see, you are no longer like you were before. Look back at your life. How you did accomplish all those beautiful things you've done already? Do you think you did it with your personality? No, your lower self can't do anything without your higher self. But you didn't know that before you were awakened. It really is the mystery of life, but now you are living it. It's simple and easy, but it took us many lifetimes to learn. We are in a deep sleep, because we became a dumping ground of the false beliefs and misconceptions of our ancestors. But now we are awakened to the truth that we are love and light. We no longer clutter our minds but instead receive

The Growing Tree of Life Inside Us

a limitless supply of what we need to do what we want to do. How simple is that?

My younger brothers and sisters, listen to me so that you can have an easy life and survive in this beautiful earth of ours. You too will awaken your children and your children's children, so that they won't fall for false beliefs or suffer without finding the light of their true selves.

Now that I have given this knowledge, I commit myself to awaken more of my other self—"you all"—if I can. How can I keep this wisdom to myself and not pass it on when the "I Am that is in me is also the I Am in you"? I can't afford not to let you taste the happiness and joy that is accessible to all who are ready to find it, and you can only find it inside of you. Once you find "me" in the stillness, I'll always be there, and you can do anything because of your love of me. I will never let you be hungry or empty-handed again.

Each one of us has different gifts, the ones you were born into, and you know them instinctively. You can feel them instantly. Once you get in harmony with your energy and the energy of all that surrounds you, you are in harmony with the energy of all that is. The universe will rush to give it to you. It's effortless because it's no longer your will working in you, but you just cooperate with it. That's the beauty of it all.

My younger brothers and sisters, why suffer so much in your life? Why travel the long road with so much toil on the ground and with sweat in your brows? You can just find me, take my hand, and never think again that you are separated from me. From then on, you will never feel tired or like a burden again, because I am the one working in you.

Is this my mission and purpose? Is this why I came to this earth? I don't have to question anymore. I'll do the best I can for each one of us to fulfil our purpose. For my second journey in this lifetime, I dedicate myself to awaken as many of my younger brothers and sisters who are ready to learn. You can only find the truth through your hearts. You have nothing to lose but all to gain because you can have an easy life with an abundance of joy and happiness. I wouldn't tell you this if I hadn't proven it myself. No one can change you, only you can.

Chapter 4 – Born Again by the Spirit

Now that you know how to do it, what are you going to do? Are you going to continue in your old ways and beliefs, which brought you nothing but hardship and no happiness or joy? If you only have the courage to try, it will pay you back all in one day. Because of you, I found my real and only self—me. How beautiful is that? No more hunger, hardship, problems, worries, sadness, anxiety, or anger Only joy and happiness while you are in the flesh. Don't you like that?

I'm telling you this because I'm here in the flesh witnessing and experiencing these things. I don't have to die. I have brought heaven here on earth and have all the good things I want because I found the real me. Heaven is within you through your heart and the feelings of love and higher vibration. That's the secret, my brothers and sisters.

I can only bring you the message, but it's up to you to do it for yourself. I continue to do what I love because, after all, love, wisdom, and power are all there is. I have to continue shining my light more brightly from day to day. Someday it will be bright enough to light the whole world. I will continue planting my seeds because I can't be bothered by the twisting storm that surrounds me. My focus is on love and light, and no one will harm me or destroy me, for my love is rooted deep under the earth, and only I can uproot it. I will continue to plant the seeds inside the hearts of everyone who can feel the message I bring because I know they have their own gifts to pursue and will become fruitful and plentiful so they can share with the world as well.

We must all wake up to the truth that we are all the builder, the dreamer, the keeper, the getter, the thinker, the giver of all that we can see in the world. By switching our mindsets together, we can change the world and bring clean air to breath, clean water to drink, and a clean ocean for all the creatures to live in the sea. We will all live a joyful and happy life in this beautiful planet. We all have a hero inside to fight for the good cause and the good for all of us. We don't only hope—we must do it together to see the result. Fight to participate in the creation of your Divine love to share with the world.

The change will begin in us individually as thousand and tens of thousands feel "me" inside of them. They can do wonders. Many of them we've never heard of before, but they will become leaders to help us carry on the work. It will happen soon because our collective consciousness is awakening now, and that's not a coincidence. Our higher self leads us all to our collective work here on the earth, and we must all recognize that.

That's why I'm here doing my part in the collective work to awaken those who are not aware of themselves yet. I hear the voice that says, "What are you worried about? You are not in charge of them. I am, me, and I am in charge of you. Will you help me so that they can feel me inside of them?" If this is my purpose in life, I will gladly do it, because it makes me happy.

Every day I walk down the street, and I never have a difficult time talking to people to influence them and help them find themselves. They may know who they really are, but once you're connected to your higher self, everything changes gradually, and all your old ways become new.

The Growing Tree of Life Inside Us

To be connected to my source is a beautiful thing. Who doesn't want to be aware of their higher self? How I wish I had known this before! I would have had access to my gift and be able to help more of my brothers and sisters access their gifts. We can all live in this beautiful earth as happy and joyful human beings with no more conflict, war, greed, or hatred. It's never too late, whether you're old or young, we can all have an impact and we must do it for our own good and life. We must not wait for tomorrow or later. "Now" is long overdue. We all must awaken to our universal consciousness that we are all "One." Once everyone awakens to that truth, we'll have no more hunger, war, killing, sadness, worries, or problems. Just an easy life of happiness.

We are born again by the spirit, by thinking beautiful things and inspiring, encouraging, and helping one another, for we are all "love and light." Humanity had forgotten that for a very long time, but now we are starting to awaken. The change is coming whether we're ready for it or not. It will come, and that's a good thing. How beautiful it is to witness the changes around the world. We have been awakened to our wrongdoing and now we are starting to make it right.

Don't be disappointed at what you're seeing around you. It will take time before we see peace without conflict, beauty without ugliness, and light with no darkness. That's why we have to change our thinking and be more positive so that our vibration will be lifted up and we can tap the knowledge of the higher dimension. We are no longer working with our will but combining with our higher self's will. This will make it easier to do the things we really want to do without losing our footing or making mistakes.

What a big change I see in my life now every day! I walk around and it's so easy to converse with people on the street. Either they start the conversation or I do. Every day, I'm able to influence some brothers and sisters by telling them the truth. They not only agree with me, but no one has told them before. It's not the teaching in their church. I don't push my thinking on them, but I open the gate of their thinking so that I can shine a light on their thoughts and give them a chance to open their minds to the truth. All they have to do is stop separating themselves from the main source.

Just as the branches of a tree wither and die if they're not connected to the trunk, so will we if we're separated from our source. Until we know who we really are, we'll remain separated from the main source and won't produce much to share with the world.

In my life, I gave more than I received, so the universe intervened and showed me the truth. I am not in charge of my family. He is—the I Am in me and the I Am in each one of us, who is the only and one self, the "Me" or " God " inside of us. How simple it that? Now that I've explained this to you, what will you do? It's all up to you. I can only tell you, but I can't do it for you. It's because the inside job and it's your job. He is asking me to help spread the word. All of you must feel him inside of you.

Those who have been given to must give, and those who have been given the knowledge must share the knowledge entrusted to them so that all can taste the limitlessness of all things.

Selflessly living your life through honesty and gratitude is your gateway to finding "Me," your higher and one and only self. Finding the inner core of our being means finding our home atlas where comfort, freedom, abundance, limitless joy, and happiness will never end.

This is why I'm writing this message to all my brothers and sisters who are ready to spiritually awaken. Please don't be afraid but have the courage to pursue it. It's the best thing that can happened to you. Continue your inner work, and if a message or idea is given to you, just act right away and don't question it, because you're heading to the good life yet to come. Share your gift with the world because you are working now for your higher self, which is the spirit. He is the one working in you, for you and he are "One" and can't be separated. We are all "One."

The Growing Tree of Life Inside Us

I'm thankful that I'm still witnessing and appreciating this beautiful life, and I'm so amazed at the progress I am making and at the awesomeness of everything I see.

Chapter 5 – Experience the Fullness of Life

Once you are awakened to the truth of who you are, everything is possible. You can do whatever you want as long as you're not destroying the law of life. You can heal yourself and others. You can be successful and free to share with all humanity. After all, we're here to experience the fullness of life. Everything we have must be left behind, but our legacy will live on forever in future generations.

Everything is energy, and it just comes and goes and changes form. Enjoy it when it comes and let it go when it's gone. We can't hang on to anything, especially money. Those who know the secret just attract it. You don't have to labor so much, as it will come to you when you really need it. The secret is that when you want money, you give away money. When you want love, you give love, and so on. It's simple but not many practice it, so they have a difficult time. Try it and you'll see how true it is.

My motto is to live and let live. For your life to be joyful, peaceful, and fruitful, always be grateful and count your blessings, because you don't know if someone is observing you. You will influence many to change their lives for the better. How beautiful is that? Lots of my co-workers told me that they have a happy life now because they followed in my footsteps. How cool is that?

How much more beautiful can their life be if they read my message and awaken themselves to their true reality? That they themselves are the way, the truth, and the life? That they are the power of everything they want in their life? Please hear me now for your own good and happiness. I wouldn't tell you this if I hadn't proven it in my own life.

Six months ago I was in the Philippines, and six months later we were in north of Spain. I'm not bragging to impress you but to prove to you how beautiful life is. If you're able to change your thinking from negative to positive thoughts, you will train your mind, and all things will follow. Trust me, I have done this, and it works.

Yesterday my husband and I came back from our twenty-three-day break to the north of Spain, Asturias. We just decide to travel there from October 1st to 23rd, without any plan at all. I thought it would be a good thing to do after finishing my other book three months earlier. When I came home from my visit to my home country for three weeks last April, I thought I deserved a little break for working that fast. Don't you think? I guess so.

I wanted to finish and publish this book as soon as I could to bring my message to the world so that they too can change their lives for the better. We can't change the world, but if each one of us can change our life, the world will follow because we are all the light of the world. So why not start shining your light brightly now? Now is the time, my younger brothers and sisters, for a spiritual awakening in which the impossible becomes possible.

You might wonder how you could fill up the blank sheet of paper with beautiful words, but it's all inside of you. Write down everything you want to tell that could help each one of us make things better, for we are all "One."

Your awareness of being, your consciousness, is the almighty Father working in you. Your work is as simple as that, because our consciousness is the only reality, and it will never die. There is no other God than "Me."

The Growing Tree of Life Inside Us

I don't mean to impose my own thinking on you, but if resonates with you, why not? People have eyes, but they can't see; they have ears, but they can't hear. I have awakened not only my eyes but also my higher eye, or your third eye that's in between your eyebrows when the time of the opening of your pineal's gland You can do the same if you try, have a courage, and don't doubt that everything can change for the better, if not for the best. Always have faith and believe in yourself because you are the only source of everything you desire in your life.

Why wait so long and continue coming and going over many lifetimes? You can do it now, and you don't have to struggle or toil in the ground by the sweat of your brow, traveling the twisting and winding roads of life. If I'd known then what I know now, I would have avoided all this trouble. That's why I'm writing this message to you, so you will know the beauty of my life now and won't go through what I did before. I struggled once, and I have given you the secret of a happy. We are one. I am in you, and you in me. I now work in my divine self to spiritually awaken more of my younger brothers and sisters. I hope that I've done my part. We are all spirits experiencing life in the flesh. We are limitless, so if I can do more than this, I will.

Whatever you desire and dream of will be given to you when you have the courage to find out who you really are. Dig deep into the inner core of your being and heart. Knock slowly that he may hear you and open the door for you so that you will know that you are the way, the truth, and the life. You are the only source of what you're looking for. In there you will know the real meaning of freedom and not being a slave but a true master of how you live your life. You also need to participate and give back, because that's the law of life.

Until you have been given the wisdom and are faithful to it, you will never know how to interpret the beautiful story of the Bible. The events never happened, but the drama took place in the mind of the mystic who wrote it in his lifetime. It's all about the universe and nature. It's about disciplining humanity to come into harmony with all that is.

The Bible is the most beautiful book ever written, and it teaches us how to behave and be disciplined in our own religion. It doesn't work for most people right now who become awaken individually, for they know that they are "Love" and "Light," and they become the light of the universe. Just look up in the dark night at the stars in the sky. How bright is your light shining in the darkness of humanity? Are you a contributor or a consumer? You have a choice, so please make it now. The world need you right, Now Jesus was our guiding light when he was walking on this earth on his life time and now he is in all of humanity as the living "Christ" and "God." We are all "One," for he is the keeper of our heart's door so that we may come into our Father's mansion with many rooms that he prepared for us in order to sup with us. Our consciousness combines with this universal consciousness that becomes "One" and all that "is."

So, my younger brothers and sisters in spiritual awakening, dream lofty dreams, and you may be like me talking to the airplane passing by and telling it to bring you somewhere someday. I told myself that one day I would find out the truth about all the religions, and it was reveal to me. You too can change your life and be the best you can be. Follow "Me," the "I Am" in you, for I am you, and I will guide you. I will tell you everything you want to know that you can't get from your teacher, your school, your minister, or anyone else. I am your higher self, your divine self, your higher intelligence. I am working with you, your Father in heaven works so you work, your consciousness

Chapter 6 – Think and Grow Rich

My husband and I arrived in Madrid on October 2nd, early in the morning. We couldn't check into the hotel yet, so we left our suitcases there and explored Puerto Del Sol in downtown Madrid. We took a bus, since we didn't have a card for the metro. In the bus, I saw a pretty woman with a little girl about four years old. I assumed it was her daughter. I smiled at the woman but didn't talk to her. She looked friendly to me.

We walked around downtown with many tourists from all over the world. We saw group tours from China, Italy, France, Vietnam, and Rome. The city was crowded with people and never-ending construction. We'd been there five years earlier, but it seemed that the construction was in the same area.

We went to the Hamon museum, which takes its name from the hams hanging throughout the place. The people stood in the middle with their drinks and tapas. The energy and vibration of the place is so intense that Fermin and I had to go upstairs for our lunch. After that we walked again and bought some fruit and breakfast to take back to the hotel.

While we were on the bus going to Chamartin Station, the same lady got on by herself. I smiled at her, and she sat down close to us. We started talking, and I asked her where her daughter was. She explained that she was actually her employer's daughter, whom she'd looked after since birth. I was surprised and commented that they looked so similar, and they were both pretty. She laughed and said that she was a Filipino and had been there for fifteen years. I told her that I was a Filipino too and was there on vacation. It's not too often these things happen twice in a day, and I was able to give her my awakening message. She laughed again and said it was funny. Because we were in the same level of consciousness, we both laughed because we both were looking for someone to talk too, which is hard to find when you're in an awakening state of mind.

My younger brothers and sisters, if you're planning to travel to Spain, please don't miss the north of Spain, Asturias. There are many towns to visit, like Santiago de Compostella Castello De Leon, the Silence Valley, Gijon, Virgen de Cobadonga in Mieres, in Leon, Valladolid, Murcia, Burgos, and so much more. The beauty of the mountain and green scenery are fantastic to look at while traveling on the train. You will feel so alive and full of life.

On October 20, we went back to Madrid for three nights and two days before heading home. But guess what—we were on the bus, again going to Chamartin Station, when this lady got on. She was surprised to see us again, as this was our third meeting. Coincidence? I know she needed me, and I needed her. We talked and exchanged our addresses and phone numbers. Hopefully we get in touch. Her name is Mary. I told her I was writing a book about my awakening, and she asked me to send her a copy.

I love the story of the laughing Buddha. A man traveled far and wide carrying all that he needed along the way. At the end of the journey he found himself as a Buddha, and all he did was laugh. It's true that I am searching for God. When I searched for myself, I found God, which is good. Now, I am the master, like the sage in the old story. The sage was a well-known person in town. Everyone respected him and believed what he said. All the people sought him for advice.

One day a lady got pregnant and told her parents that the sage had fathered the baby. The mother of the girl confronted the sage, and all he said was, "Is that so?"

When the baby boy was born, the parents of the girl brought him to the sage to care for him. He took the baby with him and did take good care of him. When the boy was about nine years old, the mother of the girl come again and explained that the daughter had lied to them, and the actual father of the boy was the butcher in the market. She asked for forgiveness. The sage just said, "Is that so?" He gave the boy back to her. After all that, the sage's reputation was ruined.

That's my example for not worrying. Whatever turmoil surrounds me, I'm at peace with "Me." What about you, my younger brothers and sisters in spiritual awakening? Do you have eyes but can't see, and ears but can't hear? Or will you say, "Is that so?" Be masters of your senses that bring trouble to your life, for you can change your negative thinking into positive thinking, and you can access your higher self. If you aware of that, everything will change for you like magic, and the magic life is yours for the taking.

The best part of my spiritual awakening is that I don't make many mistakes like before. Even the mistakes of others, like my siblings, impacted me, and I ended up solving their problems. So many things involved stress, time, money, and my health, but now it's like smoke vanishing in the air. How cool is that? Even when making decisions about anything new, all I do is smile and things turn out all right.

I am grateful to know my higher self, intelligence, God, love, or light. Whatever you call it, I will never again think that I am separated from that; instead, I am that, and that's the truth. My younger brothers and sisters in the spiritual awakening, you too can multiply your wealth. Think and grow rich like me, for we are all heirs of this limitless wealth. Claim yours, for no one can do it for you but you.

I am in you and me; he doesn't need anything because he is everything. He just uses you for his attributes. Our job is to think, dream, and desire. That's how the seeds grow in us, and it will show to the world. It's as simple as that. If you aren't conscious of it, you may not know this, and it might take you many lifetimes until you awaken to it. So why not now? You can have an easy life in this lifetime. Don't you like that? It's all up to you.

As for "Me," I have nothing to do with death and rebirth, for I am always alive in humanity. There I live and move and have my being. I have nothing to do with the shell that the meat has already taken out. That doesn't worry me at all. For nothing dies but the personal self, the ego self, the lower self, but our higher self lives on, so what's the sadness about?

I want my legacy in this life to be as a helper in opening the floodgate of crystalline light that is consciousness to millions and billions of people, for the "I Am" in me is asking me to help him in the process of awakening I do my best to write in a way so that many can absorb the message and change their way of living. I can't say that this is my last book. I'll keep on sharing, because sharing is everything.

Every time I go home to the Philippines, my friends visit me, and I greet them by saying, "Welcome to the house of a living Christ." Then I show them a picture in my iPad of a framed picture of Jesus that's by my staircase at home. I wonder if it's the actual face of Jesus of Nazareth who once walked on this earth and taught love and light and the law of "One."

Chapter 7 – Giving First and the Getting Follows

My younger brothers and sisters in spiritual awakening, until you recognize and believe the truth, your light is just sitting inside of you. Are you going to knock on the door of your heart that he may hear you and open it for you so that you can connect with your main source? Your life will be easier, and you will grow in prosperity, health, and happiness, with more options. It's all up to you.

I don't want anyone to go through my experience of struggling to survive. That's why I've been given wisdom and knowledge on how to make it easier, healthier, happier, and more plentiful. I write to awaken my younger brothers and sisters in spiritual awakening. That there is an easier way of living. Dive in and you too will never regret it. Trust me. I have been there, and ever since I've been guided by my higher self, I haven't failed.

Now I don't worry about anything. I know I am protected, and I always smile. Who will give me a sour face when I smile at everyone? All I get back are smiles, for what you give is what you get back. If you want anything, give it first and the getting will follow. That's the law of attraction. I practice that and it always works in everything. I just imagine it, and it comes. Even my religious friend, Delia, told her friends from her church that she has a friend who doesn't even go to church but has everything, and she was talking to them about me.

During my working days my coworkers often asked me what my secret was, and I told them. But they didn't believe me. I can't enforce my thinking to all of them, only to those who have eyes to see and ears to hear.

When it comes to health, we are given a guidance to prioritize what's going on in our bodies and when to see the doctor. At the same time we participate by adjusting what we put into our bodies, such as foods that are easier to digest, and we learn that we are the master of our body and health. This results in less stress and anxiety and more joy and happiness because we don't focus on the problems, so they just dissipate.

We know that all of us will transform someday, but if we can hang on for a while, we can still do some good things that will benefit everyone, especially the younger ones. After all, there's no waste, for everything is recycled, so no worries.

During my awakening, I was given a vision of three of my previous lifetimes. In one, I had a twin sister, and. We were different race as what we are now Our skin were black We weren't poor, but we weren't very rich either. We had a red car. In the second life, I was in the body of a beautiful white woman, about five-feet-eight-inches in height. It looked like I belonged to a well-to-do family because I was wearing a pink dress with a matching hat. I had a son about three years old. He was walking about a hundred meters behind me, and a lady tried to help him catch up. I turned around and said, "Just leave him; he'll learn how to live and figure out. My husband, Fermin, was in my third life, but we looked primitive, like it was a very long time ago. We were very poor, and it looked like we were somewhere in Europe, with beautiful mountains and wide-open ocean. Wherever I travel it seems like I've been there before.

We've all had many lifetimes. Yours may not have been revealed to you yet, but it will come. Isn't it amazing to think that we've been here before? But we forget. Even though I had a hard time with my parents growing up, it was easy for me to evolve and survive life as

The Growing Tree of Life Inside Us

a teenager. I was able to help my five siblings and my parents, as well as relatives and the needy people I met along the way. I always participated in contributing to their lives, even though at the time I wasn't aware of what I was doing. I was already being guided by my higher self, love, light, higher intelligence, God, Buddha, Jesus Christ. You can call it any name you want according to what you believe, but it's all "One." In this lifetime, it's been revealed to me that the "Law of Oneness" is the best thing that has happened to me. Have eyes to see and ears to hear my message to you all, for one day you will say to yourself, "I'm glad I did."

The new world is coming, and how beautiful it is to live. All of us will be the change agents of that new world. We will be the givers, the takers, the thinkers, and the dreamers. There will be no more hunger in this new world because we'll be living in the powerful experience of the spiritual awakening. We're all responsible for the life we want to live. No one can give it to us, but we have to create it by changing our thinking mindsets so we can lift up our spirits and one another in love and understanding, and helping each other create the very best in us, for we are limitless. The vast wealth of this earth is more than enough for each of us to use in this lifetime and many lifetimes to come, if only we are conscious of what we're doing to our planet.

So, my younger brothers and sisters in spiritual awakening, the I Am in you, the God inside of you, is just waiting for you to wake him up. He is you, your real self, and you should never again think that you're separated from him, for you are "One." Once you recognize that, your life will never be the same. I am the tree, and you are the branch (your lower self). Once you are connected to your higher self, the real you, the branches will never wither but will be full of fruit. You will become the source of blessing to everyone you meet, for they will recognize "Me" inside of you.

Once you find the Kingdom of God inside of you, you will become a happy, joyful person, and life will be magical. You can't wish for more, but all things will be added unto you. That's why I'm giving you this message, so that you will feel this inside of you. There's no other way to find your real self but through your hearts. Make your choice, and I'm glad you did.

Our minds are like a garden. We have to clean up our thinking and remove the negative thoughts that never help you improve your life but make it more difficult to maneuver. Like a garden, if you don't remove all the weeds, they will grow rapidly and overtake your garden. All the green vegetables you planted won't grow. You'll have nothing to harvest. Instead, we must cultivate the plants and remove the unwanted grass that grows with them so that they can grow into full blooms. Likewise, we must always be aware of what our thoughts because they can build us up or destroy us and break us apart.

Our way of thinking is the key to a good and successful life. We need courage to train our mind and change our way of thinking. If you're always thinking negative thoughts, like hate, jealousy, anger, unkindness, and ungratefulness, these will become attached to you and make it difficult to improve your life. If this is the case, change your thinking into positive thoughts and you will become those things.

Even when I was younger, I didn't have anyone to look up to for my guidance, and I knew that I didn't have the means to get an education because my parents couldn't afford it. I did everything I could think of to finish high school, even though it took me five years. I worked during the day and studied at night. There's always a means to get anything you want. You can do it when you choose to have the courage and aim for a good and successful life. I have been there, so now I can tell you about it. There is always some means to survive because we're all spirits experiencing the body, and spirits are limitless in that they don't recognize time and age.

You don't have to be scared to write about what you've been through because you'll be doing a service for humanity. If your

The Growing Tree of Life Inside Us

experience gives you a successful journey and turns your hunger into happiness and joy, you must pass it on to help others, as we are all "One." That means you have a heart and care for your other self. Don't even question if people will read your books. The important thing is that you did something of service to others as a whole. When you live without purpose, the wind can blow you away and you'll have nothing to hold on to, so please think about it.

Whatever you do is your legacy in this lifetime, so why not do it? I did mine. Those who are open minded will have the eyes to see and the ears to hear. They are the ones who benefit from my work, and I hope they will recognize that someday.

Whatever I love to do, I still want to do. If more doors open to me, I'm willing to do it. If it makes me joyful and brings happiness to me, I'll be happy to do it for the good of all, or the "One." Don't be ashamed of being old. It's a privilege. Look around ... not too many people are hanging around, and it's mostly the younger ones who are gone because of a lack of wisdom and understanding. They indulge too much in everything, like food, drink, and drugs. We must help one another open the eyes of our young ones, so that they can live their lives to their full potential.

Yesterday after doing my grocery shopping, I thought it would be nice to go for a little walk, but I was right at the bus stop when the bus came by. I got on the bus and decided to go to one of the crystals and gemstones stores. When I walked into the store, my eyes opened wide and my jaw dropped at the awesome beauty of the magical gemstones and crystals. I like to feel the energy, because these crystals and gemstones are just like us. They are alive, and their energy is in harmony with ours. They can heal us.

I looked around to see if I was attracted to some so that I could buy them and bring them home with me. My eyes were caught up in the beauty of citrine and amethyst with pyrites. They are so beautiful to look at, and all of this wealth is of the earth we are all custodian to make us inheritors of the earth's wealth.

The inexhaustible vastness of the earth's riches is courage to every one of us if we can dig deep into our conscious mind and claim it. There are many ways to find wealth if we're creative enough, and the best way is through your heart by finding the real you, your only self, "Me."

Always think big; don't stop dreaming, desiring, or doing what you really love, for those roots will sprout and become like a big oak tree—unshakable, standing tall, with the roots spreading for miles and miles. Be like that oak tree that no barrier can break and no opinion can change your decision. Your light will shine brightly like the sun, with no more shadow. The floodgates will open. That's the power of the real self if you have the courage to find it. It's not separated from you; because you come in this planet Earth, it's your soul, your consciousness, the only truth that exists in you, the real and only self of you, "Me."

Stop looking somewhere else, for you will not find it where it is not. It's only through your heart, the inner core of your being, that you can have communion with him, and everything will change in life. Keep raising your vibration through love, happiness, and joy and your thoughts will change into positive ones.

Chapter 8 – Become Clear in Life

We all are the way, the truth, and the life. No one can go to our heavenly Father but through us because heaven is not outside of you but inside of you. It's not a place you can find some distance far away but it's inside of us all. Just do the inside work and it's as easy as that. It will lead you to your Father in heaven, your consciousness, your awareness, all there is. Please do more of your meditation, where all the fishing begins.

By quieting yourself and closing the door of your mind to the intrusion of negative thoughts, you will have ears to hear all the guidance and ideas that will pop up. There will be millions of them, and you'll have some choices to make, especially regarding what you really want to do. Now you become a fisher of people, and prosperity and abundance will follow because the world is our oyster and limitless

Yesterday morning, we met a man sitting on the ground with a piece of cardboard. I wasn't able to read what was written on it, but he said good morning and something to my husband. I was behind him, so I didn't hear what he said. My husband said no as he checked all his pockets for coins.

"How are you?"

He looked at me and said, "Life is tough. I have blisters on my foot; I'm trying to control all negative thoughts, but I can't stop them in my head.

"Yes you can," I said. "You're doing the right thing now; just continue and it will happen. Who is the master ... you or your problems? Trust in yourself because you are powerful; you just forget who you are, but you are the living God. Whatever you believe is what you are. Talk to your heart in the inner core of your being. He is listening, so keep talking until he hears you. He is your real self, your higher intelligence, your only one self, the "I Am, the me" in you. It is the God in us all, and we are all "One." Just keep talking to yourself, and he will tell you everything you want to know. Trust me, it happens to me, so it can happen to you too." I extended my hand to shake his, and I said, "I have no more to give you because we are just walking and I didn't bring money, yet I give you everything I get, because I am in you, and you in "me."

My husband was just shaking his head as we moved on. If all of us were aware of little things that we could contribute to, we could make this world a better place. Be aware of those who have not, and you will be given more. You are not liquid light anymore but you are conscious, which means you are crystalline light. You have become the light of the darkness of humanity, the source of blessing to them. Open your heart to anyone and more love will pour to your heart. We are all love and light, but if you're not aware or conscious of that, you are still with the masses.

I've been working on this by myself for quite a while now, as I haven't found a community that resonate with me yet, but it will happen. The floodgate will open and be unstoppable. Every day I look for anything that gives me inspiration to do what I love, which is share more of my light with anyone I meet. If that works, it can change their life for the better if not for the best because I commit to that as my mission in "Me." What about you? Do you have any purpose for living? We all do because everything has its own purpose on this planet, even the trees and the insects. You may not be aware of it now, but it will come and it could be your "aha" moment. Now is the time that it's most needed in the world. We can all come together and help to change the confusion that's going on around us. It's not a coincidence but it was meant to happen. The universe is alive and well.

My younger brothers and sisters in spiritual awakening, just keep doing what you love because one day you will be awakened and you will look in the mirror and say to yourself, "Life is beautiful, joyful, and full of happiness." What else you need if you found "Me"? Nothing, because I am everything, and everything is mine and also yours. It's as simple as that. So life is easy.

Once you are awakened, everything you see around you and all you do has meaning. You're always moving forward and never backwards because you can't. I tried doing it myself, but it's so awkward for me now, so I don't pay attention to the things I focused on before that society taught were our responsibility but never made my life better.

Yesterday I was on the bus going for groceries when a lady got on with both hands full. She had a coffee and many bags and was having a difficult time standing and looking for her bus card. She couldn't find it. I stood up and offered to hold her coffee for her. She was so happy and thanked me. I said that my hands were free, and it was just a small gesture to help solve a problem. If we only had eyes to see how simple it is to show kindness to someone who needs it.

After that she sat down beside me, and we start talking. She told me that she was writing a book, and I asked her what helped her to write. She said meditation, but sometimes she didn't have time. I told her to make the effort because she was on the right path and one day would reach her "aha." I told her that our meeting wasn't a coincidence but was meant to give her inspiration to focus on what she loves to do. When it was time for me to get off, we both said bye. I smile when I think that my time is never wasted. That's how we learn from one another—by exchanging messages. If you don't engage, the opportunity will pass you by. Awareness is so important, as that's how we learn.

I have a friend who owns a store for ladies' clothing. We met on the street almost thirty years ago, and every time she has new arrivals, I'm always the first one she calls to give me a good price. Another friend sells jewelry. I met her around the same time, and we're still friends. Every time I visit these friends, they tell me to me pick anything I want and give me a good price. But I tell them to charge me the right price so that their stores will be here for a very long time.

Taking advantage of others isn't good. Always be fair with your dealings. Even before my spiritual awakening, I was always generous in giving to others if I could, but I wasn't aware of who controlled it all. It was the "I Am" in me, my higher self, which I am conscious of now. It comes down to our relationship to our divine source. We always harvest our intentions, whether bliss or suffering.

I do some distance healing for my family and friends, and their feedback to me is that it's working. I also teach them how to do it for themselves because everyone can do it. That's how powerful we are if we believe in ourselves.

This is our future now; we can't go back to our old way of thinking in the past. We've learned that it doesn't work and it didn't give us the abundance and freedom we wanted. The changes are coming because we're all the maker of the change, the awakened ones, the consciousness in the collective journey for the balance of everything and the benefit of all.

Each one must contribute and live purposely for that future. Our higher self is the one in charge in each of us now—not the personal self, the ego self, or the lower self. Their time has passed and gone. No more hunger, for we are all working toward that, which is why we strive because everyone can do so.

That is also why I'm telling you the truth. The God you are looking for isn't far away from you or separated from you. It is you, your real self, the "Me, the I Am" in you. Feel "Me" inside the inner core of your heart. I am there just waiting for you to recognize "Me." I am you, your real self, your higher intelligence, the universe, nature. You can call me anything you want, but we are "One." Believe, and everything I have is also yours, for "I Am" your Father in heaven calling and telling you the truth. "I Am" your consciousness and all there "is."

Is there anymore I can share to prove to you that you what I'm telling you is true? Do whatever you desire and dream of doing. See if you can prove it to yourself. It's easy because of the "I Am" in you that your ego self thinks is you, but it's "Me." I'm just using you; I'm the one doing it for you. Without "Me," your higher self, you can do nothing; the flow of life that I'm giving you is your breathing every moment. You are alive because of "Me." Don't you like to be connected to your main source?

I have completely surrendered to my higher self, love, light, the living Christ, the living God, or whatever you call it. It's "One," and it's the best thing I have done. Had I not, I would still be in my deep sleep and not doing good for the whole.

The work I'd loved doing since my younger days I couldn't do anymore. I carried the responsibility of helping my parents and siblings break from the chains of poverty, but I couldn't do it alone. I had to help them awaken to their real selves, and that alone would do the job; after all, I'm not in charge of them. A voice awakened me: "I am me, me" and "I Am in charge of you. Will you help Me so they will feel Me inside of them?" I will never forget that voice in this lifetime.

I committed myself to awakening more of my younger brothers and sisters in spiritual awakening. Feel him inside of you in the inner core of your heart. He is alive and well but waiting for you to recognize him and never again separate from him. It's you, your "real self," the light that is with you when you come to this earth, the one that guided you to find your way. It's your consciousness, your awareness that keeps changing and growing as you age. He has always been in us since the beginning of our time on this earth.

Now that we remember who we are, we have to work collectively for our own good and the survival of the next generation on this beautiful planet of ours. We must work together to save our planet so the next generation has a home to live in. We must contribute in any way we can because we are "One."

We must think collectively so that we can create a sustainable life for all. We need to change how we teach in school and heal our bodies so that we're not confined and separated or isolated. It's not impossible to create a new world now that thousands of us have already awakened to our truth. We are working with our real self, our truth, our higher intelligence in the midst of us now. We will not make any mistakes as we create the future that is "Now."

We will eradicate hunger and homelessness and create harmony all over the world. There will be no more war. We must start in ourselves and no longer be separated from our true self, our divine self, our Christ love, the living God. Believe in each one of our endeavors in life because each one must contribute their gift to the collective purposes for the good of being all "One."

I am so blessed and happy to participate and contribute my mission for the change in our way of thinking. I'm able to work in this lifetime through the guidance of the Holy Spirit, who touched my soul so I could shine my light a little brighter than before and ignite the light of many more. My younger brothers and sisters in spiritual awakening, one day my message will fall into your hands. Hear me so that your light will shine brightly too, even more than mine.

As we are growing forward little by little, we are peeling off our masks, and the time is coming when we'll have nothing left to peel. Because we are all energy we will change our form and dimension and become higher and higher as we contribute to the beauty of the whole. We will be like the seasons and the changing trees in that we can all witness the coming and going of their leaves.

Collectively, we are creating a balanced life for future generations by unlocking the door of the generous universe for the good of all. Now is the time, my younger brothers and sisters in spiritual awakening, to feel "Me" inside of you. Raise up your feelings and vibration, for these are life itself. You can do whatever you want because it's all in "Me," You can look up in the sky and see your reflection as the brightest star because of what you have contribute here on earth.

I feel so blissful and humble to be given a chance to contribute the things I really love to do. I wonder why now, but I shouldn't question that because I completely understand that "Now" is the right time. I can give encouragement and inspiration but also let them taste the happiness and joy I found in "Me" because it's endless and limitless in all parts of your body and life. Where else can you find it but inside the inner core of your being through your heart.

We can now in our collective thinking unlock the light of our love, wisdom, and power that will open the gate of the abundance and riches of the generous universe. We all become the creator of all the things that we really love to do and want to see on this beautiful planet we call Earth. No more hunger or sleeping on the street, because everyone will be awakened to who they really are, and happiness and joy will never be the same again.

We are all multidimensional creatures. We never stop working in our waking hours. As we sleep, we do our astral travel to access the other dimension, because we are all spirit and limitless.

My younger brothers and sisters who have not experienced or tasted the beauty of life—start lifting up your vibrations through feelings of love, compassion, and inspiration and soon you will find your "aha!" moment and you'll know what I'm talking about. So start finding "Me" within you, and you too will say to yourself, "I'm glad I did." Your gratitude will bring you to where you want to be.

Now that I have received my enlightenment, I've turned my focus to helping you receive yours, because that's the only way we can light the darkness in the world. It will take time, but at least we've started it, and it must go on after my lifetime. How can I turn my back on this after receiving my truth and tasting the endless happiness and joy I now own? After seven decades of walking this earth, I am able to open my gifts, which is my birthright to do, and I'm glad it didn't pass me by.

When your gift comes to you, open it right away. Don't let it pass you by because it could be a long time before it comes again. Once the universal consciousness touches you, it's hard to ignore because it plays with your hair and touches your shoulder and face. It passes by your eyes, and all you have to do is open up the gifts given to you. It's as simple as that.

I'm grateful that my gifts came to me in a simple way so that I can help open the eyes and ears of others to their truths inside of them. There they can find love, wisdom, and power just waiting to be unleashed. The floodgates will open, and everything is possible. You can make "Me" whatever you want, and it will come to pass.

Keep dreaming and desiring your mission. Keep it in your heart; guard it daily and watch it to make sure no intruder comes into your thoughts. One day it will grow and supply you with its fruit so you will become rich and live to your full potential as the happiest human being on this beautiful and generous planet Earth.

We will share our wisdom with one another and become the light in the darkness of humanity. We all have different gifts and are all guided by our higher selves to meet people who can share their knowledge and gifts with us to make our lives worth living as we pursue our own destiny with hope, love, and light. Then you too can help others open their eyes to the truth.

It's so important that we must aware and connected to our main source, the Higher Intelligence inside us.

There is a story of a young man in his forties. He became a best-selling Author and makes 1.1 million dollars. One morning he is listening to a radio station and hears this lady who's talking about how to handle other people's money through investments to her financial institutions. He is convinced and phones this lady to meet her. In short, they meet and put all his money for investment with all his trust, as not only is she a good talker, but good looking too. As the story goes, the first time he received a financial statement, he makes $ 500,000.00 out of his million. He was very please and trusts her more. Month's pass, and before he knew, out of his millions, plus the interest, only $180,000.00 is left. As you can see, she charged him $ 350,000.00 a month for service. He had a very comfortable life before this, but if you're not connected to the "I AM, ME" of

The Growing Tree of Life Inside Us

you, what you have, will be taken away. For that, he's been living in his Van with no running water.

It is so important that we must be aware and connected to our main source, the Higher Intelligence inside us.

Chapter 9 – From Old to the New

When we are awakened to our senses, it's easy to move to the next with inspiration and an appetite to do the things we love to do. We don't even notice the time it takes us to do it. That's how powerful we are. How much more powerful would we be if we worked together collectively? We could live in harmony with everybody and everything around us by not destroying but building one another up and loving each other as our own self, for we are "One." We must all and now is the time for "Peace of the land and the whole humanity." I am so happy to be alive and witness the big changes all over the world as people show that they are thinking of oneness now.

At 10:00 a.m. yesterday, the buzzer for the entrance door of our apartment building rang. It was two ladies asking if I was concerned about what was going on around the world. I told them that the change coming was from the old to the new day, and people were changing their way of thinking. If something is wrong, you have to find out the cause, and if your beliefs and way of thinking aren't giving you the life you want, then you need to do something. I said that it's about "Me" now, the me in you and the I Am. We are all "One." They liked that positive thinking, and I told them it's the truth. I could see the "aha!" moment in their eyes, and then I told them to have good day and hung up the phone.

With so many buzzers in the building, why did they press mine? Something must have guided them to me to hear my message. Many people are writing their messages to the world and becoming the light in the darkness of humanity. So many have awakened to the truth that the concerns of one are the concerns of all, for we are all "One" and living in harmony with everything that is.

Once you are awakened to your purpose in life, you don't question it. You just do it effortless and without knowing it, not like before when you had to spend too much time thinking and had many sleepless nights figuring out what to do. You had many trials and errors before you figured out what to do, but now you just do what you have to do and it's done. Most importantly, you're sharing it with the world, so that they can change their lives for the better, if not for the best. My work is the result of everyday meditation when I tap the messages from my higher self. Whatever message he wants me to write, I write.

Yesterday I went to my doctor's office and saw a young man sitting with his skateboard and holding a sign that said: "Please, I need some change because I am so ugly that no one will give me a job. They don't like me." He looked at me and smiled, and I smiled back at him and said, "You're lying. Why would you do that to yourself? Look at you. Instead of a sign you should bring a mirror with you. I will give something because I like you, and you're sitting there asked yourself, 'Who am I?' Think about it, and I'm sure you'll be surprised and will remember that you're better than this. You deserve more than this." He said he would try, and I told him to do it right now, no more excuses. I left him and heard him say, "God bless."

Little words that can give someone inspiration and awareness are a good thing. Just say something because we're all "One." What we do is our contribution to humanity as a whole, and little things are never wasted. So give it some thought, because you can change one life for the better, and it will add to your life too. Words of wisdom are given to us from deep in our inner core, and we can learn a lot more from that than we learn from our school years. You can use it right away, and it will save you a lot of time because it will be easier and you won't make mistakes. You will be happier and more joyful.

What I learn, I pass on to all so that you don't have a difficult time figuring it out. You can do all you want by healing the aches and pains in your body. Just send energy to the parts where it hurts, and happy feeling will work quickly. Believing is the key.

When we are conscious of what we're doing, our work not only benefits us personally but also the community, or even the whole world. Now it's not only our personal will but also the universal will; he has chosen us individually to work with him on whatever he wants to show in this earth for the good of all. That's what we are doing now as the new day dawns. As conscious leaders, we are working side by side to create permanent changes to build a foundation that the younger generation can maintain for their own survival in the collective purpose.

We must work together to encourage the parents of young children not to impose their own old beliefs on their children but let them choose what they want to do for a career. That will make their life easier in the future. Don't teach them about separation but encourage them to play with everyone and to help one another. Open their eyes to see what's not right because we're not separate but belong together.

We eat similar food, and we all dream of a good and better life. We all want to be happy and joyful. When we put divisions between us, we all experience tension and unhappiness. Why do we continue doing things that cause us to separate? We must change our mindset and help one another, inspire one another, and say good words of wisdom to make everyone aware that we are all "One," for the "I Am" in you is also the "I Am" in me.

As conscious leaders, we must work together to contribute some amount of money to build a community meeting place where we can all share and talk about the concerns of one another and our families. We can tell others what we lack, and everyone can contribute what they can. We'd encourage every family to have outings with their family to get a break from just working and to see some other places that will inspire them to appreciate the beauty of being alive.

Many people never travel to another country because they can't afford it. This is especially true in the Philippines, where people live and die in the one place where they spent their entire life. We will change that and give them a chance to see how beautiful our world is. They will be amazed and have an appetite to live longer.

There is no limit in the unseen world. All we have to do is dream and desire. It's happening now all over the world. All of us can do that, we just need the courage to follow and the impossible become possible. Time waits for nobody, so we will do the very best we can while we still have the time.

The old days of thinking that only a few families can gather wealth and amass riches for their generation are over. The new day has come, and the new leader has come from the spirit world to balance the activity and harmonize humanity and planet Earth. These leaders are here now to do those jobs, and we are all doing it. It's happening now right in front of our eyes. Beautiful changes are taking place and everyone must have the piece of the pie. If you think that you can't do it, first change your thoughts to "I can do that" and go for it.

After me, new and different messages will come. No one can do the work of another. What are in your thoughts now? Making a new flying machine? Creating new music? Designing a new style of homes, or new tools for farming? Growing new foods? Our consciousness has no limits, so we are all limitless.

We are the awakened generation, and we don't want to repeat the mistakes of the generations of the past. We must take care of our planet for the generations to come. Each one of us has a purpose and mission while we walk on this planet.

The Growing Tree of Life Inside Us

We mustn't take too long to figure out what to do. We can change everything so that we can live in peace, freedom, abundance, and harmony, but we must patient and respectful to the ones who are not at our level of consciousness yet.

Chapter 10 – Follow Your Heart, Believe in Yourself

We the awakened ones must work together. Time will not wait, so we must do our best to fulfill our purpose now that we have awakened to our gifts. We must do it without delay because now is the time and the new day. The new earth and the new world will arrive, and we are preparing ourselves to welcome them as they approach quickly. We are all walking the talk now and enjoying the journey. How long it will last is known by each of us individually, because each one of us is the holder of that truth. There is no beginning or ending, for the unseen to seen life must go on. Don't be wary about the outcome. It will be good, if not the best we wanted.

What a privilege to walk on this beautiful planet and leave a positive footprint. The good work we will be remembered by the next generation because we, the awakened ones, prepared for their coming. We did it to the best of our ability so that the new generation would have a good life as they continue what we have started.

My younger brothers and sisters in spiritual awakening, don't be confused by what is going on all over the world. It's a new day and a new world. We have awakened to who we really are, and we can create a family of oneness. There is no reason to be separated, for we are all one and one with our main source—the flow of life that flows through every moment of our breath and makes us alive and well.

How much more powerful would we be if we all were awakened to the truth that each of us is limitless? Once you find "Me," I will guide you to everything you need to complete what you said you would do. You will see the result with your eyes, and you will touch it with your hands. The happiness and joy will make you proud of "Me" and thankful that I kept my promise to you.

What else do you think you are capable of doing? All you want, you can do through me, as long as you aren't harming others or taking what belongs to your brothers and sisters. I am allowing you to do so because I'm sure you won't harm anyone. You know that by harming anyone or anything you harm yourself, for we are all "One." This attitude will be everywhere in the future because the Holy Spirit is in the midst of us all and in charge.

Once our individual consciousness is activated by the universal consciousness, we see everything clearly and our feelings and vibration become higher. We see things outside of ourselves differently. Things don't annoy or bother us anymore, and that's a beautiful thing. You live every day with happiness and joy that no one can explain except you alone because you live in it, and your life becomes full.

Who doesn't want that kind of life experience while in the flesh here and now? We are all at peace with everyone and everything that "is." That's exactly why I love helping to wake up the world to work together for the common good to live life in peace and happiness and harmony with all that is.

There will be no more friction, no more sour faces but only smiles from everyone you meet. You will pour love into one another through vibration and feelings, and you'll give peace and joy to everyone you pass by. Life will become easy and productive, and we can share our self-knowledge with anyone willing to learn. Once we start working with our higher self, there is no more resistance around us but only cooperation, harmony, and happiness.

Now that I've awakened to my purpose on this planet, I will use my precious time to remind my younger brothers and sisters to live happily and focus on positive thoughts and attitudes, because miracles happen every moment of our lives. The universe, the nature, the higher self, the living God, the Christ love, the higher intelligence, the light, or whatever you believe in, is always guiding us and watching us wherever we are. Don't entertain any negative thoughts. You will be surprised how true this is.

Follow your heart; believe in yourself and how powerful we are if we know who we really are. Each one of us has a powerful force inside, so wake him up. He's waiting for you to work with him. Once you're aware and conscious of that power, the beauty of life begin. This is the kind of magic life I enjoyed when I came to Vancouver at the age of thirty-one. I never wasted my time but always moved forward. I don't waste my thoughts in useless thinking, and I share all I have with my family back home and with people less fortunate that I. I'm glad I have done that because the happiness and joy inside me can't be bought with money. It's priceless and limitless.

I don't ask myself if this all there is because I found "Me," my real and only self. I feel complete; nothing is missing in my life now. I feel whole. That's the true happiness each one of us is looking for. You can't find it until you are awakened to your truth, and that will come while you are still walking here on the beautiful earth.

Just quiet your mind and breathe, imagining something you'd really like to have or do. Imagine how beautiful your life would be if you accomplish that. Is it worth doing? Will it bring you more money and happiness if you can have it? Keep dreaming and water it with inspiration and a happy and joyful attitude. You will become a dreams builder because that's how finding "Me" begins.

Once you are aware of your real self, everything is easy and more ideas come to you. If you really trust yourself, you will build a right attitude and grow more. It's not difficult compared to default living in which you struggle so hard and long and make so many mistakes you give up and lose hope.

In the past, only a few elite could access this secret society, but now any one can, including you. You can pile up wealth for your descendants, but now it's much more of a balance living in harmony with everyone and everything. That's the law of nature: we must help one another. Working together for the common good benefits everyone. It brings the new day, the new regeneration, and the new world. The awakened universe is the genius universe.

Everyone must contribute with the gifts they brought to this earth. That's your purpose for the common good of all humanity, the earth, and everything that is. We can do it. We must do it so that this earth will still be here for generation to come. I do my best to spend more of my precious time awakening my younger brothers and sisters so that they too can give to the common good of all humanity.

Be compassionate and patient with our younger brothers and sisters who are unfortunately less aware. Their time has not yet come, and that's why suffering is inevitable. But we can remind them of who they really are and how successful they will be someday. Like us, they will survive the hardship of life that we all must experience. It's not that bad, is it?

I spend my time telling you my experiences so that you don't have to spend your time making mistakes in your precious life when there's an easier way. You can have abundance, happiness, and joy inside and out. Don't you like that? I found the holy grail, the secret society, and now I pass it on to everyone so that we all can live in harmony in this beautiful earth. We are not separated from one another, but we are all "One."

We the awakened are working together to build a solid foundation for the new world to come. We are teaching one another how to do it. I am sending you this message because soon you too will contribute when you remember your purpose and mission on this earth.

Keep doing what you really love to do. Put your heart into it and don't question why, for the "I Am in you, the me in you" will guide you and do the work for you. Don't be afraid of the unknown because at the end of the rainbow, there's a pot of gold.

Don't you like that? That can and will happen to you. You will become the source of happiness, love, abundance, and healing to everyone you meet, as well as your family and friends. Wouldn't it be nice to pass on your wisdom and knowledge to them? Then they too will have an easy and plentiful life.

Chapter 11 – I Did Not Choose This Job, the Job Chose Me

What matters the most is that we spread the good news quickly before we run out of time to save our beautiful planet from sinking into the deep ocean. We must all contribute and work for all. The time of criticizing the work of others is gone, as is the time of the perfectionist. We are new builders, new thinkers. We don't hunger anymore because the clean, generous earth feeds the world with healthy food, plentiful food. Everyone teaches one another the hidden things that must be exposed for oneness to occur. Our leader is in the midst of us all, guiding us and teaching us what he wants us to do in this planet we call home.

My younger brothers and sisters in spiritual awakening, I will do my best to quicken you because that's what he is asking me to do. I will do it as quickly as I can before the time runs out. Time is passing by will and won't wait for anyone, so we all must hurry because all of us have the same time—no more, no less.

I didn't choose this job; he chose me, but I'm loving it and do it with ease because my higher self is doing it. He just uses me, so I am working for "Me."

My younger brothers and sisters in spiritual awakening, if the call knocks on the door of your hearts, don't question it. Listen to the voice of love and do what it's guiding you to do. Everything inside and outside of you will change completely. You already have a dream and plan inside of you that you've been keeping there for many years, but you don't have the courage and inspiration to take action. But when the time comes, you will surprise yourself because the wings of life will continue to flow but you won't feel any exhaustion in your body or mind. That's the river of life, and it's difficult to contain. You just go on and on until you've done it completely and amazed yourself.

We can't force things because that's how we make mistakes and spend too much time and effort with no result. We must break the silence and work together to check on our neighbors and ensure that they're safe. We must ask them about their concerns and let them know that we are ready to help them in time of need and stand shoulder to shoulder with them. If they are capable, they too must assist in helping the community wherever its needed. We will make this our priority for the sake of the happiness of everyone, and we must strive to create sources of income for everyone. Our community will need a leader who's authentic and trustworthy to be voted on by our society. Once a month we must dialogue about how the contributions are doing and how the people are responding. We will also ensure that the community's trust isn't being abused.

We must pursue and create this kind of life because that's what our universe is asking us to do—to live in harmony, peace, and happiness. We will be the awakened ones who will become solid leaders. No more excuses. We are capable of doing anything we want, and we all can help someone who wants to travel to see other countries but can't afford it. Our community will support that with everyone's help.

Someone will think this is just a dream. Yes, but we are all the builders of dreams and make them happen in reality. We are the solid dream builders for the younger generation so that they can continue our work for their children and their children's children. This world must become a better place to live.

The Growing Tree of Life Inside Us

The possibilities are endless, and everyone can tap into the reservoir of their unconscious mind, where the gold has been hidden so deep for hundreds or even a thousand years. We can bring it into the surface of our lives and watch everything change. People will comment on how lucky we are to have good fortune and an easy life and happiness. But, my younger brothers and sisters in spiritual awakening, these too can be yours if you take a few minute to quiet your mind every day.

Don't ever think that to dream is wasting time. No, to dream is to realize it, because we are all dreams builders. We can't build anything without dreams, for with dreams comes inspiration, focus, action, and then materialization. Whatever dreams you keep in your heart, water them with happy thoughts every day. The smile on your face and the high vibration of your feelings will lift you up into action one day, and you will even surprise yourself.

When you see a beautiful things in the store that you really want to have, you lighten up your face and don't worry if you have money to buy it. All you want is to have it, and there you are … you got it. That's how simple it is. It's just a matter of changing your attitude to a positive one. Always think that you are one with the main source, and life becomes so easy.

Once you know the secret, the law of life, you get used to it, and the smile will never leave your face. You'll meet people smiling at you because you're attractive to them, and you'll talk with them. That's how life becomes joyful and happy, and that's how you become the light of the world. Don't worry about money because wealth will always follow, but you must not forget gratitude and giving too.

The world is our oyster, and we must give back—first to ourself, then to our friends and family, and next to one another, our community, and humanity. And then we can say to our divine self that we didn't waste our time walking on this beautiful planet.

When my husband and I first moved out of a community where we'd lived for twenty-two years and into a new community, our apartment building faced a large garbage bin. Every day I saw this man digging in it for bottles and cans to sell. One morning when I was on our balcony, I called to him and said I had something to give him. He came over, and I gave him some cash. He told me he didn't accept money that people gave to him because he knew how to survive and make a living. I was surprised, but he was right. I was like him when I came to this country, only I didn't dig in the garbage bin, and no one gave me money on the street. I learned a good lesson from a good man. I still give whatever I can, even if it's just words of comfort to ease someone's pain. We all survive life's struggles somehow. We are always the winner, the victor of what we want. We just push forward for the gift of fortune and abundance just waiting for us at the end.

And so, my younger brothers and sisters in spiritual awakening, be inspired in whatever you love doing. The magic of life is living itself. You can create more than you can imagine, for we are all the builders of our own dreams in our own ways. Although we are all one in spirit, we are all different in so many ways. Your message and gifts are different from mine, but we can all work in harmony and peace and be the light in the darkness of humanity here and now.

We must push through, shoulder to shoulder, helping one another and learning from each other. No more hidden things, as all will be in the light for the sake of "Me." Slowly but surely, one by one, we are building our body muscle so that we can work side by side. Even when our bodies are resting, our divine selves are working non-stop. When we get up in the morning we feel exhausted because our soul has traveled somewhere else. That's why when you go to new places you sometimes remember some buildings or trees, because you've been there before and you remember it so well.

How beautiful our life is when we awaken our unconscious mind to our conscious mind. We can access a different dimension and the creative possibilities are limitless. To those who think they haven't or can't do anything, have peace in yourself and be still and know that you are God. You can become a co-creator of "Me."

I went to my doctor yesterday for a regular checkup, and she said my lab work looked good. She asked me why I looked so happy and why my eyes were shining like a star. I explain my awakening to her, and she told me that she felt something different too but didn't know what to do. I told her to focus on loving herself, believe in herself, and think positive thoughts. Be happy and loving to everything and ask herself the questions: "Who am I?" and "How can I serve?" I told her to quiet her mind and not be scared. She was pleased with these tips and said she wouldn't worry about anything.

What a beautiful feeling when you can advise someone who has no idea what happiness really is.

The time will surely come when all of us will be awakened and connected to oneness. How beautiful life will be! I'm glad it's happening now in this lifetime. The feeling of lightness and the freedom from troubling thoughts are wonderful, and that's exactly what the new world will become.

Chapter 12 – The Magic of Life Is Living Itself

What's next for me? Another door will open for sure, and I can't wait to see what that could be. I'm sure I'll be running to meet that gift so that I can share with everyone who wants it. The beauty of having my spiritual awakening is that all my needs are supplied and I don't have to think hard about any topic. All I do is just write.

We never run out of inspiration if we only look around us at the beauty of nature. From different blooms of flowers to different shapes and sizes of mountain, from the blue, deep ocean to the variety of creatures that surround us, we never go wrong looking to nature for inspiration.

To you my younger brothers and sisters in spiritual awakening, I hope that someday my work will land in your hand and inspire and remind you of something you really want to do or have in your life. Do it as soon as you can and don't put it off. The time is now, when we most need it. But we shouldn't forget that we're just passing by here. This is not our permanent home, as we will continue our journey somewhere else.

Wake up, my younger brothers and sisters in spiritual awakening, our earth is sinking, and we must all work together to clean up what we have damaged. All the creatures of the sea are dying. Find your means to contribute and do the things you love and dream of doing. Now is the time, because the help of the collective consciousness will activate your individual consciousness and make it much easier. Please just do it.

Although my vision will take much longer to materialize than my lifetime, I can at least contribute as one of the many who lead the way. Soon a community of all conscious leaders will come together and support humanity in a collective manner, not in a shadow but in the open light.

I have always been responsible, and although I didn't accumulate a mass of wealth, I have been taken care of by the higher power I am connected to. My life now is more fruitful, and I continue to grow and spread more of my light to any of my brothers and sisters who are willing to change their life for the better and lighter way—not like the lives of our parents who struggled so much.

Now it's easy for us to access the wealth we accumulated from lifetime-to-lifetime experiences, as we can mine it from our unconscious mind to the conscious mind. We find this wealth only if we have ears to hear and eyes to see. We all must find our own way to tap into, because the possibilities are endless and limitless.

My younger brothers and sisters in spiritual awakening, look around you now. So much change is going on. Open your hearts to love and light. Go for any positive thoughts or ideas that pop up in your mind, because those are the seeds of your dreams. You forget doing it in your other lifetime when you walked on this earth before. Now is the time to connect to your main source that will help you fulfill that dream.

We have to believe in ourselves to experience the beauty of our essence and everything we are capable of. The magic is in our thoughts, feelings, and the energy of our vibration that becomes our actions. Whatever we love to do will flow to us if we have an inspiration.

Just being alive and able to say hello and smile is a blessing. We get to share our happiness and joy with everyone we meet, and that will elevate their feelings, whatever their state of their consciousness is at this time. We can help to relieve the burdens of their lives.

Once we master our lower self, our ego self, or personal self, just follows in line, and our happiness and joy are unstoppable. Our appetite for living is the inspiration in all we do, which is why I focus so much of awakening my younger brothers and sisters. That's my vision here on earth.

The songs of John Lennon are coming to pass as thousands of people wake up to the truth that there is no separation but only oneness and collectiveness. Lots of jobs are vanishing, but more people are creating businesses to support their lives and prove to themselves what they're capable of. My younger brothers and sisters in spiritual awakening, whatever you do for your livelihood, do it with love and devotion, for that is what you have chosen to do while on this planet. You have never wasted your time but have contributed as a whole, so be joyful for what you have accomplished.

Be compassionate to those who are not at the level of your awakening. Be an observer but not a taker of whatever their drama is. Avoid it if possible, because there's no point explaining it to them. They won't understand you, so just change the topic or leave. Always be careful of explaining your point when they don't need it at the time, because that energy could be used in some positive way.

I haven't yet found the community that will resonate with my mission, so for now I must focus on the work my hands can do, and I know my voice will be needed when I find my community circle. It won't be long now. For now, I use my voice on a one-to-one basis, and people agree with what I'm talking about. My husband always stops me because he says one day I'll meet someone who disagrees with me and get into trouble. That's not my concern. I know who's got my back. It's important to not waste time. If your intention is pure and simple, you could help people improve their lives.

Chapter 13 – Become a Master of Your Own Thoughts

How peaceful and beautiful to live together on this planet that all of us can share and enjoy the generosity and abundance of our world. Life will become easy and fulfilled for everyone. There will be no more hunger, no more tears, no more worry, and no more problems because we will be living in harmony with everyone and everything that is.

This is possible and will come to pass because everyone wants to live that kind of life. More conscious leaders are rising up around the world, and this is what we all are working for. It will reach its peak and become easier as we help one another unlock the genius in each one of us.

Focus on and aim for your big prize because it can come at any time now without warning, and the magic will begin. Just open your eyes and ears, for it will come from outside before it's triggered inside of you. Only you can feel and explain what is happening in your inner being. I've been there, and that's why my happy face never leaves. I wish for all of you to experience that kind of life of happiness and joy that we all are searching for. For some of us it comes early in life, but for me, I waited seven decades of this lifetime and then it hit me. How cool is that? I won't forget it ever.

Now as a master of my own thoughts, it's beautiful to be free from aches and pains in my body. Just by changing my thinking the pain is gone. Even when problems come they just vanish into thin air, because I don't pay any attention to them. This is what freedom really is. We all learn to experience it as we grow, because that's the law of nature.

Most of our experiences are good, and some aren't so good, but now that most of us are awakened to the true power within our reach, we can command the sleeping giant inside to be unleashed to contribute to our survival as a human species. What a beautiful experience to be a multidimensional human being! No actions are wasted, and everything we do serves a purpose.

We must continue to do the best we can in what we love to do so that the flow of life that can benefit not only you but the whole collectively. Who says that we can't fix the problems humanity had created in the world? Who says that we can't create the lives we all want to live? It is possible because we're all working together now as a collective consciousness all over the world.

Wake up, my younger brothers and sisters in spiritual awakening. It's time to stop sleepwalking and time to walk consciously on the field of your real dreams. It's time to tell yourself to do the conscious work you love to do, and it's your purpose to do it in this lifetime.

I don't want to know if what I'm doing now is really my purpose. I don't have time to question that now. All I want is to do something that I love and contribute while I'm still walking on this beautiful planet called Earth.

Stop believing on the experience of someone else. Believe in your own experience ask yourself, "Who am I? How do I want to live my life? What is my purpose? Why am I here in this lifetime?" All of the answers are inside of you. Keep asking because it's worth it and you will not be empty-handed.

Now is the time to know and find out who we really are. We aren't children anymore, when we believed what others told us to believe. Now we are adults, and as we discover our true selves, we have a choice of how to live our own lives. We can be free from all the worries and instead be healthy, wealthy, and happy. That's all we needed. If we become this, how easy it is for us to overflow what we have to everyone we meet along the way and generously share the knowledge of oneness.

Change is coming quickly, for we are unstoppable. The conscious leaders are generously sharing because that's what we're all aiming for, and it will benefit the world. Our thoughts lead us to our feelings, which lead us to our actions. Our actions will lead us to the result we want. We are all the army of change, and we're working at full speed. The masses aren't noticing it because they're so busy sleepwalking. But once it reaches their conscious thinking, they will roll up their sleeves and work together with us, and that's how it's done.

We are human, we are all in oneness, and we are all connected to all that is. To live in oneness is to live in harmony, looking after one another, helping, and sharing. There will be no more hunger or homelessness because we know how to live in abundance and prosperity and in generosity. That's our future. We will become the pioneers of the lives we want to live in peace and plenty.

So what will you do now that you know the truth? Will you still be in doubt? Or will I see that happy smile on your face? It's your choice, and the rest, as they say, is history. Don't believe my experience; believe your own, and you will know the truth.

Chapter 14 – Forgiveness and Forgetfulness

About sickness: If you don't mention the name of an illness, or even remember it, the illness won't find you. You become what you think. So why bother? Just forget it.

I remember my grandmother on my father's side. I never saw her go to the hospital or take any medication. She never even slept in! She was always on the move, taking care of the animals and gardening, yet she lived to be 111 years old, from 1865 to 1976. What a beautiful life.

The best thing we can do for our health is to be aware of what we put in our mouths when it comes to food. Everything is good but in moderation, and I never tried smoking or doing drugs. Avoid conversations about illness, because if you listen to that old crap, your mind will get caught up in those thoughts, and you know exactly what comes next: worries and fear.

We become co-creators of what we really love and want our life to be like. We can all access the field of dreams and pick and choose what we love to become. You can live abundantly and magnificently by making yourself the source of all that you want, because you are. It's already in us, so instead of imagining it, just do it, because it will come.

In the past, just thinking about my household chores exhausted me. But now I do everything without even knowing it. What a beautiful life indeed. That's why I focus on awakening as much as I can while I'm still here walking on planet Earth at this time. I want you all to feel that happiness and joy I'm talking about. It's forever, and it's so easy and fulfilling. This message isn't new. You already know it, but I'm just reminding you because you have so much on your mind that you can't have a clarity, but everything will fall into place.

Everything we encounter in our life is a lesson to help us become stronger every day, and there's an answer to every problem. It's all inside of us so that we can deal with things quickly. When you master your mind, problems seldom come to you. They're all in our thoughts, and if you can't shake them off they become real, so don't think about it in the first place. That's how you become free.

I am thankful for the support I get from our community all over the world. That's where I find my inspiration to keep doing what I love to do, because we are not alone. We are one, whether you can accept that or not. I understand that we're not all at the same level of our consciousness and will always encounter someone who is against it. I am considerate and don't insist that they agree with me. Their time will come when they are ready. The best thing we can do is assist them if they ask for clarification, and we can talk about our experience.

Forgiveness and forgetfulness are the best attitude I ever adopted. I have lightness of heart now compared to what I carried with me for so long. Now it's gone completely. I have nothing to be forgiven of. Everything in my life is light and clear now that nothing is holding me back. Now I choose the easy way without any burden. I know the secret.

To live carefree is to live in abundance and productivity. The blessings from your life will flow to your family, the community, and the world as a collective whole. Don't wait too long to make your divine self the source of all you want to have and how you want to live your precious life, because no one can do it for you but you.

I have to be urgent in my reminder to you, as we don't have much time to wait. Our forests are burning, we are being bombarded with typhoons and flooding, and our brothers and sisters are losing everything. They need our help. Wake up, everyone, wake up! Don't sleepwalk so long that you wake up in the bottom of the ocean. Now is the time.

Feel "Me" inside of you. "I Am" your divine self, your "real self," your high intelligence, the "God" inside of you. I and you are one. Know me, find me, and be one with me. Give me part of your time, and I'll teach you everything you want to know about life. Don't separate from "Me," because I'll make your life easier for you. I will remind you of your gifts that you brought with you when you came to earth. But you forget me when you became a sleepwalker with the masses. Now is the time to wake up and remember me, for "I Am" waiting for you right now. Open your eyes to see the signs and your ears to hear my sweet little voice. All you have to do is quiet your mind and I will show you the way.

My experience is different from yours, so learn from your own experience and believe in yourself, for you are the way, the truth, and the life. You and the Father are one Your own consciousness is always with you, and it grows and unfolds in different stages of your life. Once you understand that truth, the joy and happiness will become permanent inside and outside of you.

Just vanish your doubts and believe in yourself. You are everything you can think of. You are the tools you need to become the co-creator of your beautiful life that you've wanted for so long.

By helping you, my brothers and sisters, I help myself tenfold because the flow of love in me overflows to you, because we are all connected to oneness as a collective whole. You can do the same, and all the masses of liquified light will become crystalline light, so the whole world will become a shining bright light as one. Who doesn't want that? No more shadow but just bright light.

All the conscious leaders all over the world are preparing to usher in the coming of a new world, a new day, a new now, and the regeneration of a new generous and abundant world, all will be guided by the spirit in their minds. There will be no more tears or hardship, only ease, joy, and happiness. That's how the spirit wants us to live.

Chapter 15 – This Is the End of Being Selfish

When we change our mindset from the old to the new way of thinking, life becomes simple to manage. Our mind is clear and it's easy to choose what we want out of life. Health and happiness can be reached by everyone who wants to. Many of our brothers and sisters become millionaires by teaching others how they reached success. Making millions is good because you can help so many people who really need it.

We will not turn our back on anyone who need us. That's why we're living in oneness now. Be prepared, my younger brothers and sisters, for a big change. Learn how to tap the power inside of you, for he has been waiting for a very, long time.

How beautiful life is as we learn along the way. I have met so many people in their eighties and nineties who don't have a clue about who they really are, and that's why we all inherit the darkness of this earth. It's up to us, the conscious ones, to awaken our elders and younger brothers and sisters who have no interest in finding their real selves. Those of us with the courage to dedicate our precious time and efforts to awaken them must move quickly.

Many books had been published on this, but usually the message doesn't even reach us because most of us have no money to buy the books. But now, because of my courage and the desire planted in my heart to find the truth, it was given to me.

When you're happy, you are constantly being inspired and you can have lots of ideas. That's how co-creation happens. You become energetic and light in everything you do, and it seems so easy. You have no thoughts in your mind but the work gets done. I know it's difficult to believe, but lots of people are experience it now.

My niece sent me a message last week. She was crying because, according to her, her mother just snapped without warning. She started throwing things, even the purse she'd bought for her. Her mother said it was smelly so she threw it away. They took her to the hospital because she was talking nonsense. I told her to calm down and explained that her mother was maybe going through the spiritual awakening. Lots of people go through that kind or event but in different ways. I told her not to worry and that I'd send her my healing every day until she came back to her senses.

They kept her in the hospital for two weeks and monitored her. I told my niece to have peace and love in her heart, and most of all faith that she would get better. If you awaken to your consciousness, you know what to do and can do all kinds of good things to save lives instead of panic and worry.

On January 6, 2020, they sent me a picture of my sister, her husband and their two grandson They were all smiling while leaving the hospital, and my sister looked fantastic, like nothing had happened to her. Always believe that when the darkness comes, the light must follow. Don't dwell on sadness and worry, for the light will come even more brightly.

I told my niece that my advice was not only for her mother's spiritual awakening but also for her, because it was a sad and scary event to witness. Now she learns from me how to handle things. It's time for her to think about some ideas that she can earn money with, like her paintings. Always give some thought to extra hobbies because someday they could bring you wealth. That's how the universe gives us a nudge to disturb our comfort zone so that we wake up and remember our gift.

I've been learning how to evolve and grow since I was four or five years old, and I've never stopped growing. I'm now seventy years old and still growing and moving forward, not backwards. I remember my gift that I brought with me to this earth a long time ago. It was to ignite in each of you the light so that you too will find your power, which is sleeping in your inner core. Find me within and you will not be empty-handed.

I'm sure you'll be delighted when this message reaches you because you've been working so hard and thinking about how you can improve your living condition and earn some extra income. This will be your road map, and it's so easy to follow if you have patience to learn. It works for me, and it works well. That's why I can say proudly to myself and all of you that I am one of the many people who live in happiness and joy and feel full in this lifetime.

We come to earth to learn how to survive with happiness and joy. Why settle for merely surviving? We are all come from the spirit, so we are all limitless. You can do whatever you want in "Me." So stop and think and move forward; as long as you follow the law of nature, no one can harm you. This is the end of being selfish, as each one is awakened to the truth of who they are. We all must use our inner light to ignite more light so we all can shine brightly.

We all must get out of the box because there's no room for all of us. We must live in the open space with no restriction. We need freedom to choose how we want to live our lives in peace, generosity, abundance, and good health, free from sadness, worries, stress, and problems. We should experience only happiness and joy because that's what the spirit wants for us.

My brothers and sisters, stop feeling like you are a small grasshopper in the land, for we are all big people living in the land of milk and honey. Make your choice and your action will follow. You are on the way to prosperity in your lives.

We all must help together, for if only a few are helping, it's not enough. We must first awaken them from their deep sleep, because the masses are still a sleepwalking and lazily waiting for the pie to drop from the sky. This attitude will lead them into poverty and destitution. But when they are awakened to the truth of who they are, they will awaken to their dreams and their higher potential that they have never tapped before. Then the changes will begin.

We must have patience and let them wake up first. Then the job will begin. Once they find out how easy, happy, and joyful life is, they will want to produce more to taste the fruits of their labor. They will start working together and sharing knowledge, contributing as a whole.

We cannot lie to ourselves, for that is not how the divine spirit works. It speaks the truth; the divine spirit is not partial to anyone. They can choose to work with whoever they want, regardless of education, race, or other physical features. I am often reminded of what I'm supposed to do as my contribution to the collective whole while I am still walking on this planet. So, I do it, and I hope this is it.

Chapter 16 – Standing on Our Own Two Feet

No one can give my gift to me. I must claim it for the sake of "Me." It comes once in my lifetime and never again. I don't want to wait for hundreds or thousands of years. So this is my gift, to help you my younger brothers and sisters in spiritual awakening, to enlighten you that you are not who you think you are. You are more than that, because we are all divine spirit experiencing the body. I hope that I can ignite the light of many people before my time is up on this planet. I know that' what I come here to do, and I don't question it.

Wake up, my brothers and sisters, and ignite that fire inside of you so that you can see your desires and hold them in your hands. Abundance and prosperity can be yours now. The momentum of inspiration will build into action, and that's how your magic will begin. Have courage and strength, for tenacity is a must in order to reach your goals. Heed my words, my younger brothers and sisters in spiritual awakening, because your wealth is hiding from you but it will not take long for you to discover it. You are on your way to riches in every part of your life.

There is always time to accomplish what we want in life because we all are the co-creators of what we have and what we have not yet created because the universe is a generous giver if we have the right mindset. Being conscious of what we really want must be our focus. I accomplished all of my goals and thought I didn't have any more projects, but then I remembered my purpose and mission, and that opened a new door.

Focusing on freedom was the best thing I ever did for myself. I am free to be happy and joyful in whatever I do. I focus solely on my happy life that I neglected for so long. Financial freedom is also key. When we are financially free, we can think about our goals, which are limitless. Our true self is unaware of time and works day and night, without rest or feeling exhausted. He or she uses our bodies whenever we're ready to work. It's easy if you understand it.

Because our words are our truth, we must be very careful when selecting them because sooner or later they will come back to us. Always be mindful of the good things that you want to come to your life; only entertain the positive ones and not the negative ones so that you don't encounter suffering in your life. Although we came here to learn and survive, we still must be mindful of all we do. Sometimes we are curious about something, and that's how we learn from our mistakes. As long as there aren't too many, we don't have to suffer too much. All we can do is stand on our own two feet, learn a lesson from our mistakes, and move on to do it right.

Chapter 17 – How to Find Freedom

We are all looking for freedom. People travel everywhere looking to be free. But until they stop and think about it, they will never find it because they don't know what kind of freedom they want, and they're looking in the wrong place. But once they stop and look inside their inner core through their hearts, they will change their minds. Everything will change inside and out. Their eyes will be opened, and they will hear clearly. It will be easy for them to hear the voice of their higher self, the God inside of them that is always there.

I was in this state for a very long time, but now I can tell you that there is a way so that you won't have to wait as long as I did to taste the beauty of freedom and life.

We have been programmed by our old way of doing things, but I broke free of that chain, and that's how I found freedom. You too can be free by changing your habits and doing things a new way, your own way, as long as you're not destroying the law of nature. It will cost you nothing, but you gain everything. I mean everything—happiness, joy, health, wealth … you name it and it's yours. But of course, your goals, actions, planning, and execution must follow. How simple and easy is that?

Nothing I have said is new. I'm just reminding you of what you already know. These are my experiences. How you experience it depends on you because we are different individuals. How you find your real and higher self is entirely up to you.

Inspiration comes from everywhere and even from places you don't expect. Usually it comes from our happy thoughts because when we quiet our minds, millions of thoughts come from the spirit that is all of us, which means we can do anything we want. If we want it, we become the father and the virgin mother who bears our beloved dreams, and sooner or later we see it with our eyes and hold it on our hands.

What will you contribute? Have you found your purpose yet? Do you have your mission? Don't sleepwalk for too long, because no one wants to wake up in a dark place.

Chapter 18 – Practical Knowledge

Don't ever forget that I am with you, wherever you are and whatever you do. I am always there with you because we cannot be separated and never will be. Because "I Am" you, you will never be alone. I am with you when you go to your office, to the shop, when you wash your laundry … everywhere.

So, my younger brothers and sisters in spiritual awakening, how clear is it to you now? If you still don't believe "Me," experience it for yourself. You don't have to go anywhere but through your heart; find "Me" there, and you will be glad you did.

The younger you are when you start a relationship with "Me," the better you become, and the easier it is for "One" to teach you. I will teach you everything your heart desires. You can just say the words, and I will give it to you, but you must find "Me" first.

When you look in a mirror, say "I love you" to yourself as often as you can and make it your habit. You will notice the outcome quickly, and your life will become lighter.

Look in the mirror closer and focus your eyes for a few minutes and you'll see something different: it's "Me," your real self. Talk to "Me" but select the words carefully. Make sure it's what you really want to happen in your life because I will give it to you.

You will become healthier, happier in your relationship with your family and others, and more generous to the less fortunate people you encounter. And you will increase in abundance of everything because you've become the source of all the blessings. You will be a healer to the sad and the sick because your presence and words will become their medicine. They won't see your personal self but "Me" in you, as well as "Me" in them. That's why you will never be alone if you can recognize "Me.".

Forget the mistakes of the past and make them a blessing and a gift. Turn it all around and make it great now that you learned a lot from "Me." Who else do you think you can learn from if not "Me"? It's all about "Me," my dear one.

Why take the long and winding road to riches When you already know that you are the only way, the truth, and the life, the "I Am," your only Father in heaven. I am always in you. Your "consciousness" is "Me," and I am in charge of you, everyone, and all things.

I allow you to know "Me" now, to remind you that you have a purpose and mission. That is why you are here walking on earth during this lifetime. Follow "Me" and I will give you rest while you are still in the flesh. You will live your life in happiness and abundance. Soon you can create something wonderful. You will know it because it's your dream. "I Am" the one in you who will bring you inspiration, and as you move into action, you will materialize it.

Chapter 19 – Create Something That Will Last Our Lifetime

Our intention, purpose, and mission are how we start to create something that will last our lifetime not only for ourselves but for all humanity to taste the fruits of our labor. It's not ours to keep but to share and give. We are like the fruit trees and the flowers that never get tired of bearing fruit and blossoms for everyone to enjoy and be happy. That's how we participate in the beauty of the circle of life on earth. We are all wearing different masks in different stages of our lives, different characters depending on where God put us.

Enjoy the ride and hold on tight because the very best of us will come at the best time. You are so special, just like everyone else. We are all created equal, so we are all capable of doing the very best. So, my younger brothers and sisters in spiritual awakening, what will you bring from inside to world? I'm anxious and excited for you to come out into the open. We all need you to heal the earth and humanity.

Everything is broken apart, so we must work together to make it whole again. That's why I gave you the gift of finding "Me," so that you can spread the word and all humanity will feel "Me" inside their hearts too. The truth has to come out and be open to the light.

Everyone who finds "Me" is no longer silent. They send their messages in different ways, and "I Am" allowing that because that's their gift too. I welcome any way they can help "Me" wake up people. All must participate now, as it is the right time.

It's been such a joy for me to contribute to the alleviation of the hopelessness of humanity. Ask for help, as we are ready to share our knowledge and wisdom. For we are all connected to one another and working toward "Oneness."

Always listen to people who are giving you advice to help you change your way of thinking, especially those who have improved their lives. That's how I educated myself, as I knew my parents couldn't give me a higher education. I travel, I listen, and I open my eyes and ears to learn, and all without spending too much money.

Always pretend not to know in order to know. That's how you gain knowledge. Be humble and learn a lot. That's how you become professional in everything you want to know.

When the going is tough, just keep moving forward, not backwards, because the change comes quickly. Never give up, because something big will happen. Your divine self will never abandon you, so what are you afraid of? Shake up that power inside you and the magic will begin.

Once you can manage your mind, no more hardship will come. Everything will be easy to handle. Your freedom is a given, and you can use it anytime you want to. No one is limiting you but your own beliefs. Life is abundant and limitless, and we are all spirits experiencing a body. We are all limitless, so just clear your mind and open your eyes. Harness it, as it's just under our noses, as close as our breath.

Miracles are everywhere, but you have to believe it to have it. Belief is a power in life itself. Thoughts and feelings are life and power, so be very careful how you use them because they will give your results both ways. Make sure you use them positively.

Don't worry, the time is fast approaching. Every conscious leader is working endlessly to help awaken the world for the common good. Awaken to the divinity of who you are, as the distribution of wealth from the generous universe is now. Wake up and claim yours, as no one will do it for you. Come and join us, for the time is now.

If you can only feel and see the vastness and boundlessness of the wealth of your dreams that you have kept in your heart all this time, you could bring them out. If you have the courage and take action, you will have the bounty of everything your heart desires, and you will be content all your life.

Be still like a mountain, flow like a river, know that "I Am" God and that "I Am" you. If you get that, you will live with "Me" in paradise. How beautiful it is to know the truth, nothing but the whole truth! Heaven has been here all along, and we never knew it.

Chapter 20 – Friends and Foes Are All the Same

Friends and foe are all the same, so help them if you can. Don't be concerned if they give you some heartache; someday they'll realize the truth. They are just learning their lessons of their journey on the beautiful planet Earth The heart that is forgiving is the one from which love overflows and never runs out. And more blessings will come.

We can only change the life of someone else if they can see how we changed our own. So be a good leader and they will follow your example, no harm done. Eventually everyone will grow and expand with their awareness. Everything that happens to us, good or not, is to teach us and provide experiences from which we can pick and choose. We are all passing by on this planet; the more good deeds we do, the more examples we leave behind for younger generations to come.

Until we know who we really are, it's takes a lot of effort to get out from our comfort zone. We always go back to our familiar routes. But when we have the courage to change our belief system, everything becomes clear. You don't have to worry about anything. Once you pay attention to loving yourself first and meeting your needs, everything just comes into place, starting with your overall health, joy, and happiness. You become stronger and younger again, full of life. If you give, make sure that you give the same amount that you get so that it doesn't become unbalanced and unhealthy. That is the secret to a beautiful living experience. If you think you've sacrificed too much for your family and friends, and all the other people you've helped, don't worry. The time of your receiving will surely come. If not now, later, but it will come.

I don't know why I was hand-picked by the collective unconscious of the universe to do this work, but I don't have to understand everything. All I have to do is awaken my brothers and sisters to their spiritual awakening because they are very far behind, and we the conscious leaders don't want them left behind.

Wake up, everyone! We must work together to save our planet so that our children's generation has a place to live. Wake up to know who you really are—the builder of your longtime dreams. We are all dream builders, and our future is in our hands. It's our purpose-driven life, our mission to contribute as one.

What a beautiful life when you discover who you really are. Everything change inside and out, and it never looks the same again. The thoughts that keep you awake at night are gone when you are changed by "Love." How powerful it is to live in joy and happiness, where everything is accessible to you effortlessly. Nothing could make your life better. This is why I work to awaken my younger brothers and sisters in spiritual awakening, so that they too will remember their gifts and purpose and contribute in the collective spirit. The latest stage of my life is about harvesting the fruit of what I have sown in my younger days, and I have only just begun.

I have to remind myself from time to time of the revelation: "What are you worried about? You aren't in charge of them, 'I Am,' and I am in charge of you. Will you help "Me" so they can feel "Me" inside of them." It's my time to receive the fruit of my labor.

Chapter 21 – Recognize "Me"

The secret of powerful living is inside of us. All you have to do is bring it out and start building your castle. Live abundantly in every part of your body, and the rest is history.

Go where there are no pathways, blaze your way and make your own trail, and at last you can see your footprint in the sand. If anyone else can do it, so can you, just plunge into whatever you really want to do and watch yourself become a dream builder. Action without knowledge is useless, and knowledge without action is futile.

God gives you the "Idea," and you do the rest. All the things you want start with your thoughts, and then you build your castle here on earth because you can. Believe in yourself, have courage; choice and action go hand in hand. And at last, freedom and happiness will come from health and abundance.

Why make your life complicated when it's so simple and easy. Just open your eyes and ears—abundance is everywhere. Start with your breath and connect with your higher self, your higher intelligence. Recognize "Me" and make yourself a main source of everything you really want. That's how powerful you are.

We all came from our ancestors thousands upon thousands of years ago, and here we are. We survived and will continue to survive, whatever life throws at us. So be strong and courageous, because you are. Rewire your brain by saying things like, "I will make a difference in the world" or "I can do it, and I will do it." Repeat that for five minutes every morning when you wake up and five minutes before you go to sleep at night until it registers in your mind and becomes habitual thinking.

It will take time to change your mindset, but it will happen because you can do it by repeating these thoughts. When you find yourself thinking things you don't want to think, switch quickly to what you want. That's how to do it easily. It's all in your thoughts, so change your thinking to all that you want, and it will be attracted to you. I know it will take time to train your mind, but once you master your mind, you will master many things in your life. Just enjoy the process and it will come.

My younger brothers and sisters in spiritual awakening, I have given you lots of ways and means to transform your life for the better, if not for the best. See how simple and easy it is? It has been inside of you all along, but you've been traveling far and wide looking for it. Aren't you happy now? I'm sure your heart is beating fast for joy and happiness now that you know "Me" as you, but not you as your personal self. And yet you and I are "One." And that's only the beginning. I will show you more of the beauty of you and your life that's been waiting for you for so long. Just continue on the path you're on now, and soon you will find what I have in store for you. Everything is in your hands. As long as you don't break the law of life or nature, all delight is yours to enjoy.

My younger brothers and sisters in spiritual awakening, it's time for you to remember the gifts you brought with you when you came to this earth. I want you to shine brightly in this world because you are love and light in the darkness of humanity. Bring it on. Now is the time. Wake up, wake up my loved one, you are so behind now.

So from now on, my younger brothers and sisters in spiritual awakening, rewire your brains by believing in yourself, and your higher self will gladly give you all that you want because you deserve to have it.

The Growing Tree of Life Inside Us

Bring consciousness to your daily life and it will lead to happiness and peaceful living with everyone and everything around you. If we all do this, we will live in harmony with no more hunger or homelessness because helping and sharing will be our way of life if we practice "Oneness." The conscious leaders are leading us and opening the door, awakening more of the humanity.

Whatever you do, try your very best to contribute your share to the whole, because that's why we're here—to work together as "One."

Chapter 22 – Respecting the Rights of One Another

Time is running out quickly, so we have to double our effort to work together to save our planet and clean up the mess we created. We can't wait for long, or we know exactly what will happen to us all. We don't want to go down that road. That's why I'm on this journey to help awaken more of my younger brothers and sisters in spiritual awakening. It's better to be high above than to wake up on the bottom of the deep ocean.

If we all will work together, we can prevent this darkness. We are all light and love, so we don't have to let the darkness fall upon us. We can live in the bright light. It's brighter than the solar light because we are all good humans working in "Oneness."

Individuation is the starting point, and we will support all the courageous ones who are protecting our decent way of living. They are protecting our freedom and dignity as human beings living by the law of light and love so that no one is above the other, for we are all "One." By respecting the rights of one another, we all can live in harmony and peace.

The time will surely come, and what a beautiful planet that will be! Aren't you excited, my younger brothers and sisters in spiritual awakening? It's in our hands to make because it's possible. What are you waiting for? I've started mine. What is your passion, your contribution, your purpose, your mission? Dig deep inside the inner core of your being through your heart where you can find "Me," the real you. A beautiful, abundant, peaceful, and harmonious life is waiting for you. It's all in your hands, my dear one, if you but recognize me. If you are in doubt, just ask how you can serve me and all your fellow creatures. In that moment, you will be with me in paradise.

Until you search for more and reach out for me, you won't find your mission. But if you ask me, I will guide and show you what you really desire to do. Then I will lead you to a greener pasture of your own choice, and it's right there within your reach. For those of you who are thirsty and hungry, come and know me and I will give you rest. And very soon, I will pump you up with energy and make you unstoppable. You will know that "I Am, me," the real you, the light and love, with your inner being.

You are the special one who can make wonderful things and awe others. You can be the sound of inspiration and courage to all who meet you. You become the light to the darkness of humanity. Awareness of little things can become big things. To be conscious is being alive, making less mistakes and doing the right thing for the good of oneself and the goodness of all. The ordinary one becomes the extraordinary human.

Chapter 23 – Taste These Blessings Yourself

I'm doing the work that is at hand, and never again will I allow it to slip away from my sight. This has been one of my dreams since my youth, but I couldn't find the time to write my book because I was so busy helping my parents, siblings, and other people who needed me. But here I am, now doing the work that I love. It's never a waste of my time.

It's hard for me to explain what I've experienced, so I want you to experience it for yourself. I'm not selfish, so I want you to taste these blessings yourself. By knowing who you really are and believing in yourself, you can discover more and help the collective whole.

Wake up, wake up, my younger brothers and sisters. The new evolution is here. We must welcome and embrace it with love, light, and courage. We must support one another and work together hand in hand. Our planet needs us, and our humanity needs us more. Please embark to this journey of awakening the world. For this is who we are now, no turning back. We must create a new earth, a clean earth, full of compassion, love, light, generosity, and abundance. Only we humans can do it. It's the life we all want, and it's possible because we're all doing it now.

The old ways are crumbling in front of us. Everything and everyone must be exposed to light, for there can be no more shadow, no more hidden faces. We are all working towards oneness through collective consciousness. Tear off the masks you've been wearing for so long exchange them for a smiley face that can bring happiness and joy to everyone you meet, and they might change their ways. Small gestures bring your influence to others, and the change begins.

Seek your truth first, and once you find it, you become unstoppable in making all you want come to you. The easiest way to train our brains to adopt new habits is to give them positive information, like "I want to make a difference in the world," or "I am healthy, happy, and wealthy." Our brains can easily adopt these suggestions.

We have already been programming our minds for years, but it takes time to break our old habits. But it can be done with patience and focus. Try the best you can, because you won't regret the outcome, and the very best of you will follow.

Chapter 24 – All One in Spirit

We all come from spirit and are experiencing life in the body, so we are all energy that never stops flowing, and we never stop growing. New things are always coming, our consciousness is always unfolding, so we must be ready for that. Because there is no such thing as forever.

Replay, rewind, and reset your brain, and you will get results in minutes, and your environment will change completely. All the things you couldn't see before will be clear now, and you will do things without making mistakes. All the negative thoughts will be gone. That's how you remember all the good things that you've been dreaming about having in your life. You'll have the courage to act, and you'll wonder how did you did it so quickly. that's the beauty of awakening, to be conscious and aware.

You will prosper quickly because you will attract what you want: friends, good health, and good relationships with everyone, even your foes. All negative things will abandon you, even problems won't visit you anymore. If this isn't what you call happiness, then what is?

Once you have momentum, you will never stop. You will become like a fruit tree—naked in the winter, growing leaves in the spring, bearing fruit in summer, and feed us that fruit in the fall. And the roots are miles and miles far and wide. I am inspired when I look at nature, and it makes me unstoppable. What about you, my dear readers? Where do you get your inspiration? Maybe from the vast, blue, deep ocean, or maybe from looking at little ants who are busy with nonstop gathering and piling up of their food. Wherever you get your inspiration, the main thing is that you get your momentum.

Higher education is essential for the benefit of all, and it's a gift for those who can afford it. We are very thankful for their contribution. All of us will find our way and our permanent happiness, joy, and abundance in life. You found "Me" in you, the God inside you, the love inside that lightens all your endeavors, the real you, your higher intelligence and self. You thought you were separated from "Me," but you never were.

Chapter 25 – The Truth That Has Been Revealed to Me

When you look around, everything seems so chaotic, and you can't trust anyone. But don't worry, when things settle down, all things will be clear and bright. We are all working together for the good of the whole, and no one will be left behind. We are all "One," and we can progress faster when we all work together collectively.

All things will be brought to light, and then we will live in peace and harmony, and the abundant life will begin. The spirit in the midst of us all is in charge, and if we just cooperate with it, things will be all right again. So, my brothers and sisters, don't panic or lost your hope. Just work with all your hearts at what you love to do because that's your purpose and how you can contribute your share to the whole.

Once we know who we are, we begin to notice that we are stronger than we thought we were before. Our thoughts and thinking change quickly. We no longer entertain the thoughts that kept us from improving our lives. We now focus our thoughts on all the good things that bring happiness, joy, and prosperity as we serve one another. We don't think for ourselves only but for oneness, and that's a good thing indeed.

All the thoughtful leaders are working so hard and fast, and we must cooperate to lighter the work for all. We will see the results of our good work, and by encouraging one another, the bright light of the goodness of each of us won't be hidden anymore. It will be brighter than the sunlight and will come soon.

This is the truth that has been revealed to me. What are you worried about? "You are not in charge of them, I Am, me, and I am in charge of you." Will you help me so that they can feel Me inside their being? This is all about fairness, and each one of us is responsible for the one conscious self. More revelation will come to each one because no one is left behind.

This will be the new normal now. We must use it, the new now. We must be guided by the universal consciousness that's ruling us now. Everything will become sustainable for our future, and everyone will contribute as a whole. I am so excited to witness the beauty of it all—the joy, the happiness of each one of us when we meet on the street, all smiling. How good is that?

My younger brothers and sisters in spiritual awakening, keep your hands busy at whatever your dreams are, because sooner or later you'll have it in your hands and see it with your eyes. It will start within you, by changing your thoughts, without you noticing it. You don't have to travel far and wide; it's there in your own back yard. Don't force yourself; just be aware that you are the source of your dreams, and the time will come with your inspiration that you will be unstoppable. You will become the brave one, in harmony with the universal collective consciousness.

Be joyful and happy in every minute of your day, and that's how you can accomplish so many things you want to do. Say "I love you" to everyone you meet, even if just silently. When you do this, you're saying "I love you" to yourself, because they are all your other self, as "One," and they contribute to your own happiness, joy, and lightness in whatever you do.

If we keep thinking, we won't stop growing and expanding but will become the source of the many things we think of. Make sure that you think about good things that you really want, because the opposite can manifest too. This is how simple it is to become successful—just keep thinking of all the good things and that's you will become. If you need money, don't think of scarcity, and money will just flow to you easily. If you share some ideas, more ideas will pop-up in your mind. So be aware, because the universe is listening.

Train your mind to serve you, not destroy you, because it's capable of anything you feed it. It will break you or build you. A smiley face brings thoughts of pure love and forgiveness, but a sour face is unfriendly and reveals a mind full of worry and no regards for anyone else.

Please don't harm anyone, great or small. We all have the right to live on this beautiful planet, so make your mark as clean as you can, because we're just passing by. Be gentle with yourself. Stand back and think of how you've made it until now and are still rising. How amazing you are! After all you've been through, you survived. "I Am, me" did this, yet you don't recognize me: your real self, your divine self, your higher intelligence. I am the real you. Don't forget me from now on.

Chapter 26 – Please Don't Harm Anyone Great or Small

I am thankful for my past experiences, for they molded me into what I am today. They taught me how to survive and live on this beautiful planet Earth with a better life. I will pass it on to you, my younger brothers and sisters in spiritual awakening. I will remind you that you can make yourself the source of all that you love and all want to have in your life. It's just a matter of your beliefs managing your mind and rewiring your brain to think new thoughts of all the good things you've been dreaming of. See it in your mind's eye and you will hold it in your hands.

By changing ourselves and our lives, we can work together and change the world, the one all of us want to enjoy in peace, harmony, sharing, and caring for one another. We want to experience abundance, health, and freedom from the bondages of life.

All things are easy to acquire when we are aware and conscious of who we are. Once we manage our minds, we become powerful masters of ourselves, and we can do amazing works of wonder. Self-knowledge is must because no one will teach you this at school or church. It's inside you to know. It's your truth that you can experience and only you can explain the magic of how you feel. Trust that feeling and experience because that's truth. Once you experience that, you can say that the rest is history.

What are you going to do with me now that I am growing and expanding inside of you? I am the river of life. Do you have any idea how to bring me out so you can share me with the world? What is your desire? Your dream? I'm just waiting for you to birth me. And now is the time.

Now that you know how to be a good master and captain of your own ship, why not live in limitless and boundless freedom where you can imagine and love and have wisdom and power because these are all in you. Start talking the walk that will take you farther into wider, greener pastures.

Why not shout out at the top of your lungs so that more of your younger brothers and sisters will awaken with awe in their faces to follow "Me," for it is me who has been asked to help.

Now that I've brought this message to you, it's your time to make your life and live in abundance because it's in you to make and give. Don't say that I didn't remind you ahead of time. What a beautiful and magical life. It's really being born again. It's not a religion to follow but the unfoldment of our consciousness and inner growth. The endless happiness and joy can bring you to a higher level of consciousness, where few have been before.

I don't impose my experience on anyone, but I remind them that what I am enjoying now is also accessible to them—the peace and tranquility, abundance in every area of life, the freedom to do what I want for the good of me and all. I am able to help and give to anybody who needs my help.

Once you experience that beauty inside of you, you become unstoppable. That's how you start the momentum of tapping into the source, and you become the source of everything you create and want in your life. I am so excited for you now that you know this.

Whatever you're doing now, give the very best of you with love and dedication, freedom and satisfaction, joy and happiness, abundance and beauty. You don't have to waste your time searching anywhere else because you have found your purpose. You have no more regrets. You don't miss anything in your life. You just share your passion and love with the world, and they too can change their lives because of you.

I am so humbled to have been given the privilege to write these messages to you, because the time is now and I don't want you all to fall away from your awakening but to taste the gifts of your awakened soul.

Make yourself stand out among the crowd and let them notice you for how special you are among the many. You are able to bring all those wonderful things to the world because of "Me." The floodgates must open to know the truth for the whole world to see, and no more secrets will be hidden. "I Am" your consciousness unfolding before your mind's eye, and all the things you couldn't see before are now clear to you. It's "Me" who did all this for you because it's been so long. You have forgotten "ME," and I won't allowing that anymore.

These are my message to all who want to hear me. I won't speak in parables so that you can understand right away. That will ignite the fire inside you so you will stop and think of all that goodness hidden inside. Bring it out for the world to see, and share the beauty of you. The wealth and abundance of all the good things you can create are within. No one can do it but you. With courage, strength, focus, resiliency, tenacity, joy, and happiness, you will bring your mission to the world. You will become the brave one who has the discipline to create all the good things you've been dreaming of your whole life.

Until you know who "I Am, me," and believe that "I Am" the real you, and that "Me" and you are "One," your life will never satisfied or fulfilled. Be humble so that I will count you and accept you to work into my vineyard. Even if you come late, your salary will be the same as the first one who come Because you follow "Me" and never abandon "Me," I will guide and protect you all of your life; instead of testing you, I will continuously bless you. Everything you touch will bring life to you. I am here to supply you with all you want because you never fail to love me, serve me, or recognize me. You will never again be separated from "Me," or the "I Am" from all.

I hope you enjoyed reading my writing and finding your love of living in abundance, peace, joy, and happiness, full of gratitude, love, and light throughout your lifetime.

Until we meet again, have peace in all the days of your life.

Inocencia Tupas Malunes

01/05/22

CPSIA information can be obtained
at www.ICGtesting.com
Printed in the USA
BVHW081457031221
623140BV00001B/5

9 781039 121836